THE
ACTIVE
INTERVIEW

JAMES A. HOLSTEIN
Marquette University
JABER F. GUBRIUM
University of Florida

Qualitative Research Methods
Volume 37

D1041582

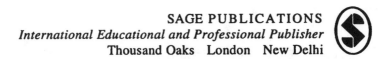

SAGE PUBLICATIONS
International Educational and Professional Publisher
Thousand Oaks   London   New Delhi

For information address:

SAGE Publications, Inc.
2455 Teller Road
Thousand Oaks, California 91320
E-mail: order@sagepub.com

SAGE Publications Ltd.
6 Bonhill Street
London EC2A 4PU
United Kingdom

SAGE Publications India Pvt. Ltd.
M-32 Market
Greater Kailash I
New Delhi 110 048 India

Printed in the United States of America

Library of Congress Cataloging-in-Publication Data

Holstein, James A.
　　The active interview / James A. Holstein, Jaber F. Gubrium.
　　　　p.　　cm. — (Qualitative research methods; v. 37)
　　Includes bibliographical references.
　　ISBN 0-8039-5894-3. — ISBN 0-8039-5895-1 (pbk.)
　　　1. Interviewing.　2. Social sciences—Research—Methodology.
　　3. Social sciences—Fieldwork.　4. Social sciences—Language.
　　I. Gubrium, Jaber F.　II. Title.　III. Series.
　　H61.28.H65　1995
　　300′.723—dc20　　　　　　　　　　　　　　　　　　　95-5766

　06　07　08　09　15　14　13　12　11

Sage Project Editor: Susan McElroy

For Lida, Z, Spud, and the Cake.

CONTENTS

SERIES EDITORS' INTRODUCTION

Face-to-face interviewing, the common denominator of qualitative research, is as difficult to describe as it is to accomplish. Field-workers are taught that success hinges on a clear understanding of the intellectual purpose of the inquiry, a talent at creating rapport, a sensitivity to the structure of situations, a sense of timing, and so forth. The synergistic influence of these factors on research certainly merits our attention.

But, as is pointed out by James A. Holstein and Jaber F. Gubrium in Volume 37 in this Sage series, much more is required of the interviewing ethnographer than the ability to skillfully pose questions, empathize, and listen.

The Active Interview takes a constructionist perspective on the interviewing process and interview products. Holstein and Gubrium are dissatisfied with the orthodoxy that interviews are usefully regarded as opportunities for enterprising scientists to mine minds. They reject the notion (so often hidden in the way we think of survey research) that crisp answers to clean questions can be recovered with professional dispatch once the ground rules are explained by the interviewer to the respondent.

To Holstein and Gubrium, interviews are social productions. With this orientation, respondents are better seen as narrators or storytellers, and ethnographers are cast as participants in the process. Working together, the interviewer and narrator actively construct a story and its meaning. Interviewing, then, is inherently collaborative and problematic.

The Active Interview is a welcome addition to the Sage series because it provides a vocabulary that helps us to think about—indeed discuss—the interactive aspects of interviews.

—Marc L. Miller
Peter K. Manning
John Van Maanen

THE
ACTIVE
INTERVIEW

JAMES A. HOLSTEIN
Marquette University
JABER F. GUBRIUM
University of Florida

1. INTRODUCTION

Think of how much we learn about contemporary life by way of interviews. Larry King introduces us to presidents and power brokers. Barbara Walters plumbs the emotional depths of stars and celebrities. Oprah, Geraldo, and Donahue invite the ordinary, tortured, and bizarre to "spill their guts" to millions of home viewers, and intimates and experts tell the "O. J. Simpson Story" for TV and the tabloids.

We live in what has been called an "interview society" (Silverman, 1993). Not only the media but human service professionals and social researchers increasingly get their information via interviews. Some estimate that 90% of all social science investigations exploit interview data (Briggs, 1986). Interviewing seems to be the universal mode of systematic inquiry (Hyman, Cobb, Feldman, Hart, & Stember, 1975), as sociologists, psychologists, anthropologists, psychiatrists, clinicians, administrators, politicians, pollsters, and pundits treat interviews as their "windows on the world."

Typically, those who are curious about another person's feelings, thoughts, or experiences believe that they merely have to ask the right questions and the other's "reality" will be theirs. Studs Terkel, the consummate journalist qua sociologist, says he simply turns on his tape recorder and asks people to talk. Of his brilliant interviewing study of attitudes and feelings about working, Terkel (1972) writes:

> There were questions, of course. But they were casual in nature . . . the kind you would ask while having a drink with someone; the kind he would ask you. . . . In short, it was a conversation. In time, the sluice gates of dammed up hurts and dreams were open. (p. xxv)

As unpretentious as it is, Terkel's image of interviewing permeates the social sciences: "prospecting" for true facts and feelings residing within. Of course, there is a highly sophisticated technology that tells researchers how to ask questions, what sorts of questions not to ask, the order in which to ask them, and the ways to avoid saying the wrong things that might spoil the data (Fowler & Mangione, 1990; Hyman et al., 1975). But the basic model remains similar to the one Terkel exploits so adroitly.

The image of the social scientific prospector casts the interview as a search-and-discovery mission, with the interviewer bent on finding what is already there inside variably cooperative respondents. The challenge lies in extracting information as directly as possible. Highly refined interview technologies streamline, standardize, and sanitize the process, but, despite their methodological sophistication, they persistently ignore the most fundamental of epistemological questions: Where does this knowledge come from, and how is it derived?

Social researchers generate massive data by asking people to talk about their lives; results, findings, or knowledge come from conversations. Although these conversations may be variously configured as highly structured, standardized, quantitatively oriented surveys, as semiformal guided interviews, or as free-flowing exchanges, all interviews are interactional events. Their narratives may be as truncated as forced-choice survey answers or as elaborate as life histories, but, in any case, they are constructed in situ, a product of the talk between interview participants.

Most researchers recognize interviews as social interactions, but the literature on interview strategy and technique remains primarily concerned with maximizing the flow of valid, reliable information while minimizing distortions of what the respondent knows (Gorden, 1987). The interview conversation is thus framed as a potential source of bias, error, misunderstanding, or misdirection, a persistent set of problems to be minimized. The corrective is simple: If the interviewer merely asks questions properly, the respondent will emit the desired information.

This approach, however, continues to treat the interview conversation as a pipeline for transmitting knowledge. A recent "linguistic turn" in social inquiry—an interest shared by poststructuralist, postmodernist, constructionist, and ethnomethodological perspectives—has raised a number of questions about the sheer possibility of collecting knowledge in the manner this approach presupposes. In varied ways, these perspectives hold that meaning is socially constituted; all knowledge is created from the action taken to obtain it. This further suggests that what passes for knowledge is itself a product of interaction (Cicourel, 1964, 1974; Garfinkel, 1967). Treating interviewing as a social encounter leads us rather quickly to the possibility that the interview is not merely a neutral conduit or source of distortion but rather the productive site of reportable knowledge itself.

Sociolinguist Charles Briggs (1986) argues that the social circumstances of interviews are more than obstacles to respondents' articulation of their particular truths. Briggs notes that, like all other speech events, interviews fundamentally, not incidentally, shape the form and content of what is said. Aaron Cicourel (1974) goes further, maintaining that interviews virtually impose particular ways of understanding reality on subjects' responses. The emerging lesson is that interviewers are deeply and unavoidably implicated in creating meanings that ostensibly reside within respondents (see Manning, 1967).

Cicourel (1964, 1974) goes on to offer insightful and nuanced suggestions for how to make sense of typical interview interactions. Briggs (1986) focuses more on how to pose questions in ways that are appropriate and meaningful to respondents, acknowledging that question-answer exchanges both provide a context and call on cultural assumptions and local linguistic practices. Elliot Mishler (1986, 1991) presents the contextual and narrative complexities of the research interview, suggesting that narrative itself is cultural. These authors all point out the need to develop better understandings of the meanings that are being conveyed in practice by both interviewer and respondent, either to avoid misunderstandings or errors of interpretation or to cast interpretation as a social construction in its own right.

This points to a significant oversight in the typical approach: Both parties to the interview are necessarily and unavoidably *active*. Each is involved in meaning-making work. Meaning is not merely elicited by apt questioning nor simply transported through respondent replies; it is actively and communicatively assembled in the interview encounter. Respondents are not so much repositories of knowledge—treasuries of information awaiting excavation—as they are constructors of knowledge in collaboration with interviewers.

This book argues that all interviews are interpretively active, implicating meaning-making practices on the part of both interviewers and respondents. We contend that if interview data are unavoidably collaborative (Alasuutari, 1995; Holstein & Staples, 1992), attempts to strip interviews of their interactional ingredients will be futile. Instead of adding to the long list of methodological constraints under which interviews should be conducted, we take a more positive approach, proposing an orientation whereby researchers acknowledge interviewers' and respondents' constitutive contributions and consciously and conscientiously incorporate them into the production and analysis of interview data.

The book presents a perspective—an implicit theory of the interview—more than an inventory of methods. We are not suggesting that the "active" interview is a distinctive research tool; instead, we use the term to emphasize that all interviews are reality-constructing, meaning-making occasions, whether recognized or not. We offer a social constructionist approach (cf. Berger & Luckmann, 1967; Blumer, 1969; Garfinkel, 1967) that considers the process of meaning production to be as important for social research as the meaning that is produced. In other words, we think that understanding *how* the meaning-making process unfolds in the interview is as critical as apprehending *what* is substantively asked and conveyed. The *hows*, of course, refer to the interactional, narrative procedures of knowledge production, not merely to interview techniques. The *whats* pertain to the issues guiding the interview, the content of questions, and the substantive information communicated by the respondent. We return to this dual interest in the *hows* and *whats* of meaning production throughout the book.

Our perspective is clearly influenced by ethnomethodology and related approaches (see Garfinkel, 1967; Heritage, 1984; Pollner, 1987;

Silverman, 1994). In many significant ways, it also resonates with methodological critiques and reformulations offered by an array of feminist scholars (see DeVault, 1990; Harding, 1987: Reinharz, 1992; Smith, 1987). In their distinctive ways, ethnomethodology, constructionism, poststructuralism, postmodernism, and some versions of feminism are all interested in issues relating to subjectivity, complexity, perspective, and meaning construction. As valuable and insightful as these approaches are, they tend to emphasize the *hows* of social process at the expense of the *whats* of lived experience (cf. Williams, 1958/ 1993). We want to strike a balance between these *hows* and *whats* as a way of reappropriating the significance of substance and content to studies of the social construction process. Although the emphasis on process has sharpened concern with, and debate over, the epistemological status of interview data, it is important not to lose track of what is being asked about in interviews and, in turn, what is being conveyed by respondents. Too narrow a focus on *how* tends to displace the significant *whats*—the meanings and cultural material—that serve as the relevant grounds for what cultural studies critic Paul Willis (1990) would call the "symbolic work" of asking and answering questions.

This book offers some observations that are quite unconventional by most social science standards. As an explication of the theoretical and epistemological underpinnings of interviewing practices in general, it is more a conceptual sensitizing device than a formula for conducting a particular kind of interview. Consequently, the book might be of special interest to researchers seeking to better understand how interview data are produced and interpreted. Its procedural implications might prove especially useful in designing, executing, and interpreting interview studies that focus on meaning-making—both its process and product.

Taking the activity of all interviewing as our point of departure, the book discusses how the interview cultivates meaning-making as much as it "prospects" for information. In subsequent chapters, we locate this active view in relation to more traditional conceptions (Chapter 2) and examine alternate images of the subject behind the interview respondent (Chapter 3). We then discuss the complex bodies of experiential information that provide participants with resources from which they formulate responses (Chapter 4), showing how interviewers establish interpretive parameters for forthcoming exchanges and shape the way issues are addressed and answers are assembled (Chapter 5). We proceed to

6

illustrate how participants link observations, experiences, and concepts to produce horizons of understanding for what is said (Chapter 6) and explore the ramifications of recognizing the multiple voices that can constitute the interview (Chapter 7). Finally, we conclude with a re-thinking of standard methodological concerns in relation to the active interview (Chapter 8). Our discussion begins by situating the active interview in relation to more conventional understandings.

2. THE ACTIVE INTERVIEW IN PERSPECTIVE

Interviews vary in several important ways. C. A. Moser (1958), for example, distinguishes them along a functional continuum. At one end, he places interviews whose purpose is to interrogate, help, educate, or evaluate respondents—as in employment interviews or police investigations. Such inquiries are conducted with decidedly practical goals in mind. Interviews with more abstract or academic goals, like large-scale social surveys, occupy the opposite end of the continuum. Eleanor and Nathan Maccoby (1954) classify interviews according to how "standardized" they are, referring in part to whether an interview is guided by structured questions and an orientation to measurement or is more flexibly organized and aims to uncover subjective meanings. John Madge (1965) contrasts what he calls "formative" with "mass" interviews, categorizing them according to whether the respondent "is given some sort of freedom to choose the topics to be discussed and the way in which they are discussed" (p. 165). Formative interviews include the nondirective interviews favored in Rogerian counseling (see Rogers, 1945), informal interviews, and life histories. Most large-scale surveys fall into the mass interview category. By and large, classification centers on the characteristics and aims of the interview process, with little attention paid to how interviews differ as occasions for knowledge production.

The Imagined Subject Behind the Respondent

If only tacitly, there is always a model of the research *subject* lurking behind persons placed in the role of interview respondent. Considering the epistemological activity of the interview requires us to ask how interviewers relate to respondents, as imagined subjects, and to the conversations they have with those subjects. (Equally important, of course, are considerations of the subject behind the interviewer, to which we will turn later in the book.) Projecting a subject behind the respondent confers a sense of epistemological agency on the respondent, which bears on our understanding of the relative validity of the information that is reported.

In conventional approaches, subjects are basically conceived as passive *vessels of answers* for experiential questions put to respondents by

7

interviewers. They are repositories of facts and the related details of experience. Occasionally, such as with especially sensitive interview topics or with recalcitrant respondents, researchers acknowledge that it may be difficult to obtain accurate experiential information. Nonetheless, the information is viewed, in principle, as held uncontaminated by the subject's vessel of answers. The trick is to formulate questions and provide an atmosphere conducive to open and undistorted communication between the interviewer and respondent.

Much, if not most, of the methodological literature on interviewing deals with the nuances of these tricky matters. The vessel-of-answers view cautions interviewers to be wary of how they ask question, lest their manner of inquiry bias what lies within the subject, which otherwise is available for truthful and accurate communication. It offers myriad procedures for obtaining unadulterated facts and details, most of which rely on interviewer and question neutrality. For example, it is assumed that the interviewer who poses questions that acknowledge alternative sides of an issue is being more neutral than the interviewer who does not. Researchers are advised to take this into account in formulating interview questions. The successful application of such procedures elicits truths held in the vessel of answers behind the respondent. Validity results from the successful application of the procedures.

In the vessel-of-answers approach, the subject is epistemologically passive, not engaged in the production of knowledge. If the interviewing process goes "by the book" and is nondirectional and unbiased, respondents will validly emit what subjects are presumed to merely hold within them—the unadulterated facts and details of experience under consideration. Contamination emanates from the interview setting, its participants, and their interaction, not the subject, who, under ideal conditions, serves up authentic reports when beckoned to do so.

What happens, however, if we enliven the image of the subject behind the respondent? Construed as active, the subject behind the respondent not only holds facts and details of experience but, in the very process of offering them up for response, constructively adds to, takes away from, and transforms the facts and details. The respondent can hardly "spoil" what he or she is, in effect, subjectively creating.

This activated subject pieces experiences together, before, during, and after occupying the respondent role. As a member of society, he or she mediates and alters the knowledge that the respondent conveys to the interviewer; he or she is "always already" an active maker of meaning. Because the respondent's answers are continually being assembled and modified, the answers' truth value cannot be judged simply in terms of whether they match what lies in a vessel of objective answers.

From a more traditional, scientific standpoint, the objectivity or truth of interview responses might be assessed in terms of *reliability*, the extent to which questioning yields the same answers whenever and wherever it is carried out, and *validity*, the extent to which inquiry yields the "correct" answers (Kirk & Miller, 1986). When the interview is viewed as a dynamic, meaning-making occasion, however, different criteria apply, centered on how meaning is constructed, the circumstances of construction, and the meaningful linkages that are assembled for the occasion. Although interest in the content of answers persists, it is primarily in how and what the subject/respondent, in collaboration with an equally active interviewer, produces and conveys about the subject/respondent's experience under the interpretive circumstances at hand. One cannot expect answers on one occasion to replicate those on another because they emerge from different circumstances of production. Similarly, the validity of answers derives not from their correspondence to meanings held within the respondent but from their ability to convey situated experiential realities in terms that are locally comprehensible.

The active approach to the interview is best put in perspective by contrasting it with more conventional approaches. We offer two exemplars that differ considerably in their orientations to the experiential truths held by the passive subject. One approach, which David Silverman (1985, 1989, 1993) argues reflects Enlightenment sensibilities, orients to the rational value of what is communicated. It focuses on the substantive statements, explanations, and reasons with which the respondent articulates experience. We use Jean Converse and Howard Schuman's (1974) unusually candid book *Conversations at Random* as an exemplary text. The other approach, which, in Silverman's words, reflects Romanticist sensibilities, orients to the purportedly deeper and more authentic value of the subject's feelings. The emphasis here is on sentiment and emotion, the unadulterated core of human experience. We use Jack Douglas's (1985) book *Creative Interviewing* as an exemplar.

The Survey Interview

Converse and Schuman's book considers the survey interview "as interviewers see it." The book is based in part on the responses to the interview process of 150 graduate students trained in survey methods through the University of Michigan's Detroit Area Study. Professional interviewers from the Survey Research Center also contribute their observations, generally by way of "thumbnail sketches" written on the last page of questionnaires.

The book's candidness comes in its unwitting juxtaposition of two distinctly different images of the subject behind the survey respondent. On the one hand, we are introduced to the preferred vessel-of-answers image of the subject. However, a contrasting image also filters through the book, hinted at from the start when the authors write, "We make no apology for the subjective nature of this material—it is the *raison d'être* of the book—but we emphasize that it is not intended to stand in opposition to more objective research on the interviewing process" (p. vii).

The book richly illustrates how interpretively engaging, and relatedly difficult and exasperating, the survey respondent can be. It describes the interesting and complex personalities and meanings that interviewers encounter while interviewing, depicting them as "the pleasure of persons" and "connoisseurs of the particular." But the authors caution the reader that, even though it will be evident throughout that the respondent can be quite interpretively active, this does not work against objective information. This information, the reader eventually learns, is derived from the repository of knowledge that lies behind the passive respondent. The authors do not believe that the respondent's conduct implicates his or her subject in the construction of meaning. As lively, uninhibited, entertaining, and difficult as the respondent might be at times, his or her passive subject ultimately holds the answers sought in the research.

Converse and Schuman present interviewers who have given considerable thought to the possibility that respondents represent interpretively active, not passive subjects. One graduate student interviewer mused about whether the respondent could be a different kind of subject than assumed by social scientists:

One begins to wonder—could it be that these alternative conceptualizations of reality [offered by the respondent] may have some grain of truth? Could it be that those values, different from mine, may be as legitimate as mine? Sitting in the university, one can see the limitations inherent in the social locations of other people and their perceptions of social reality. But one wonders, too, if the perceptions of the objective social scientists are not bounded by their own, but similar, limitations. (Converse & Schuman, 1974, p. 8)

The authors credit the insight of this novice interviewer, but, alas, it is an unseasoned wisdom. This is not the professional interviewer commenting, but the beginner who brings "an enthusiasm for new experience as he learns (or relearns) something about the wider world beyond the university" (p. 8). The young interviewer's wonderment is his own, interpreted as referring to how amazingly revealing the interviewing experience can be about the social world beyond the academy.

Although Converse and Schuman grant that survey interviewing involves experiencing the pleasure of persons, the authors hope that interviewers use their roles to effectively access the vessel of answers behind the respondent. Their book is replete with anecdotal reminders of what interviewers must learn to keep that vessel of answers in view and the respondent on target. In part, it is a matter of controlling oneself as an interviewer so that one does not interfere with what the passive subject is only too willing to put forth. The interviewer must shake off self-consciousness, suppress personal opinion, and avoid stereotyping the respondent. Learning the interviewer role is also a matter of controlling the interview situation to facilitate the candid expression of opinions and sentiments. Ideally, the interview should be conducted in private. This helps assure that respondents will speak directly from their vessels of answers, not in response to the presence of others. The seasoned interviewer learns that the so-called pull of conversation, which might have an interpretive dynamic of its own fueled by the active subjectivity of both the respondent and the interviewer, must be managed so that the "push of inquiry" (p. 26) is kept in focus. Ideally, the cross-pressures of conducting inquiry that will produce "good hard data" are managed by means of "soft" conversation (p. 22).

Throughout, Converse and Schuman's book provides glimpses of how problematic the image of the passive subject is in practice. The rich illustrations repeatedly tell us that interviews are conversations where meanings are not only conveyed but cooperatively built up, received, interpreted, and recorded by the interviewer. The veteran interviewer learns to manage the pressures of conversation for the purposes of inquiry, and orienting to an active, meaning-making occasion seems to be a mere epistemological step away.

Creative Interviewing

Compare Converse and Schuman's (1974) approach with the Romanticist view exemplified in Douglas's (1985) book *Creative Interviewing*. The word *creative* in the title refers primarily to the interviewer, not the respondent, and, according to Douglas, derives from the difficulties he encountered attempting to probe respondents' "deep experience." Douglas writes that in his many empirical studies, especially his investigation of the experiences of beautiful women, he repeatedly discovered how shallow the standard recommendations were for conducting research interviews. Canons of rational neutrality, such as those Converse and Schuman espouse, failed to capture what Douglas calls his respondents' "emotional wellsprings" and called for a methodology for deep disclosure.

Douglas's difficulties relate as much to his Romanticist image of the passive subject as they do to shortcomings of standard interviewing technique. Like the image of the subject behind the survey respondent, Douglas also imagines his subjects to be repositories of answers, but, in his case, they are well-guarded vessels of feelings. The respondent authentically communicates from an emotional wellspring, at the behest of an interviewer who knows that mere words cannot draw out or convey what experience ultimately is all about. Standard survey questions and answers touch only the surface of experience. Douglas aims more deeply by creatively "getting to know" the real subject behind the respondent.

Creative interviewing is a set of techniques for moving past the mere words and sentences exchanged in the interview process. To achieve this, the interviewer must establish a climate for *mutual* disclosure. The interview should be an occasion that displays the interviewer's willingness to share his or her own feelings and deepest thoughts. This is done to assure respondents that they can, in turn, share their own thoughts and feelings. The interviewers' deep disclosure both occasions and legitimizes the respondent's reciprocal revelations. This, Douglas suggests, is thoroughly suppressed by the cultivated neutrality of the standard survey interview. As if to state a cardinal rule, Douglas (1985) writes:

13

Creative interviewing, as we shall see throughout, involves the use of many strategies and tactics of interaction, largely based on an understanding of friendly feelings and intimacy, to optimize *cooperative, mutual disclosure and a creative search for mutual understanding.* (p. 25, emphasis in original)

Douglas offers a rather explicit set of guidelines for creative interviewing. One is to figure that, as he puts it, "genius in creative interviewing involves 99 percent perspiration" (p. 27); getting the respondent to deeply disclose requires much more work than obtaining mere opinions. A second admonition for engaging in "deep-deep probes into the human soul" is "researcher, know thyself" (p. 51). Continual self-analysis on the part of the interviewer, who usually is also the researcher, is necessary, lest the creative interviewer's own defense mechanisms work against mutual disclosure and understanding. A third guideline is to show a commitment to mutual disclosure by expressing an abiding interest in feelings. Referring to a neophyte creative interviewer who "has done some wonderously revealing life studies," Douglas writes that the creative interviewer is "driven by . . . friendly, caring, and adoring feelings, but adds to those an endearing, wide-eyed sense of wonderment at the mysteries unveiled before her" (p. 29).

The wellsprings tapped by creative interviewing are said to be emotional, in distinct contrast with the preferred rational image that filters through Converse and Schuman's book. In Douglas's inimitable style, he writes that knowledge and wisdom are "*partially* the product of creative interactions—of mutual searches for understanding, of soul communions" (p. 55, emphasis in original). Whereas Douglas's imagined subject is basically emotional, this subject, in the role of respondent, actively cooperates with the interviewer to create mutually recognizable meanings, paralleling what interviewers' accounts in Converse and Schuman's book suggest. In this regard, the mutuality of disclosure—the "creative" thrust of creative interviewing—mediates, adds to, and shapes what is said in its own right. What Douglas does not recognize, however, is that this admittedly active subject could constitute the wellsprings of experience in rational or other terms, not necessarily emotional ones. Thus the subject behind Douglas's respondent remains an essentially passive, if creatively emotional, fount of experience, not unlike the respondent who "opens up" while having a drink with Studs Terkel.

The Active View

Nearly 4 decades ago, Ithiel de Sola Pool (1957), a prominent critic of public opinion research, wrote on the 20th anniversary of the founding of the journal *Public Opinion Quarterly*:

> The social milieu in which communication takes place [during interviews] modifies not only what a person dares to say but even what he thinks he chooses to say. And these variations in expression cannot be viewed as mere deviations from some underlying "true" opinion, for there is no neutral, non-social, uninfluenced situation to provide that baseline. (p. 192)

Pool went on to describe how the dynamic, communicative contingencies and constructs of the interview literally activated opinion, so that, as he put it, "every interview [besides being an information-gathering occasion] is an interpersonal drama with a developing plot" (p. 193).

Pool's metaphor conveys a far more active sense of interviewing than is traditionally conceived. His sense of the interview helps situate our own vision of it in relation to the approaches exemplified by Converse and Schuman's and Douglas's texts. Highlighting the activity of all interviewing, the subject behind the respondent is not captured by either Enlightenment or Romanticist sensibilities. The subject is neither a repository of opinions and reason, nor essentially a wellspring of emotions. He or she is not predefined but is instead constructed in relation to the ongoing communicative contingencies of the interview process. From the time one identifies a research topic to respondent selection, questioning, and answering, and, finally, to the interpretation of responses, interviewing is a project for producing meaning. Although the imagined subject behind the respondent is eventually conceptualized, perhaps as a rational or an emotional agent, the image emerges as part of the project, not beforehand. Within the interview itself, the subject behind the respondent is fleshed out—rationally, emotionally, in combination, or otherwise—in relation to the give-and-take of the interview process and the interview's broader research purposes. As Pool intimates, the interview and its participants are constantly developing.

Two kinds of communicative contingency influence the construction of the active subject behind the respondent, which affect how responses are interpreted. One kind is substantive—the *whats* of the enterprise. The focus and emerging data of the research project provide orientation and framing resources for developing both the subject and his or her responses. For example, a project might center on the quality of care and quality of life of nursing home residents (see Gubrium, 1993). This might be part of a larger project relating to the national debate about the general purposes and organization of home and institutional care. If interviews are called for, participants add to the substantiality of these topics in their own right, linking the topics to biographical particulars in the interview process, thus producing a subject who responds to, or is affected by, the matters under consideration. For instance, a nursing home resident might, in an interview, speak animatedly of the quality of care in her facility, asserting that "for a woman, it ultimately gets down to feelings," echoing Douglas's emotional subject, articulating a recognizable, if not universally accepted, gender linkage. Another resident might coolly and methodically list her facility's qualities of care, never once mentioning her feelings about them. Offering her own take on the matter, the respondent might state that "getting emotional" over "these things" clouds clear judgment, implicating a different kind of subject, more like the rational respondent portrayed in Converse and Schuman's text. Particular substantive resources—such as the common cultural link between women and feelings or the traditional cultural opposition of clear thought and emotionality—are used to form the subject.

This brings us to the other kind of communicative contingency—the hows of the interview enterprise. The standpoint from which information is offered is continually developed in relation to ongoing interview interaction. In speaking of the quality of care, for example, nursing home residents, as interview respondents, not only offer substantive thoughts and feelings pertinent to the topic under consideration but simultaneously and continuously monitor who they are in relation to the person questioning them. For example, prefacing her remarks about the quality of life in her facility with the statement "speaking as a woman," a nursing home resident informs the interviewer that she is to be heard as a woman, not as someone else—not a mere resident, cancer patient, or abandoned mother. If and when she subsequently comments, "If I were a man in this place," the resident frames her thoughts and feelings about the quality of life differently, producing an alternative subject. The respondent is clearly working at how the interview unfolds.

The hows of the interview are not arbitrary, nor one-sided. The subject is interactionally constituted in relation to the developing contexts of the interview. Activated as ultimately rational, for example, the subject becomes a narrative resource for both the interviewer and the respondent, a guidepost for how to ask and answer further questions. In this context, the interviewer has grounds for asking about the concrete "reasons" for, not feelings about, the respondent's evaluations of the nursing home, and the respondent calls on his or her "reasoning" subject to provide appropriate responses.

The Active Interview as Interpretive Practice

To say that the interview is an interpersonal drama with a developing plot is part of a broader claim that reality is an ongoing, interpretive accomplishment—a matter of practice. Ethnomethodological sensibilities underpinning this position draw our attention to the interactionally artful methods—the *hows*—through which meaning is produced and made visible (Garfinkel, 1967; Heritage, 1984). From this perspective, interview participants can be likened to practitioners of everyday life, constantly working to discern and designate the recognizable and orderly parameters of experience. But meaning-making is not merely artful, as if those concerned build meanings "from scratch" on each interpretive occasion. Rather, interpretation orients to, and is conditioned by, the substantive contingencies of interaction—the *whats* of everyday life.

In our approach, reality is constituted at the nexus of the *hows* and the *whats* of experience, by way of interpretive practice—the procedures and resources used to apprehend, organize, and represent reality (Holstein, 1993; Holstein & Gubrium, 1994). Active interviewing is a form of interpretive practice involving respondent and interviewer as they articulate ongoing interpretive structures, resources, and orientations with what Garfinkel (1967) calls "practical reasoning." Linking artfulness to substantive contingencies implies that whereas reality is continually "under construction," it is assembled using the interpretive resources at hand. Meaning is not constantly formulated anew, but reflects relatively enduring local conditions, such as the research topics of the interviewer, biographical particulars, and local ways of orienting to those topics (Gubrium, 1988, 1989; Holstein & Gubrium, 1994). Those resources are astutely and adroitly crafted to the demands of the occasion, so that meaning is neither predetermined nor absolutely unique.

But interviews hold no monopoly over interpretive practice. Why, then, is interviewing an especially useful mode of systematic social inquiry? The answer lies in the interview situation's ability to incite the production of meanings that address issues relating to particular research concerns. In the conventional view of interviewing, the passive subject engages in a "minimalist" version of interpretive practice, perceiving, storing, and reporting experience when properly asked. Our active conception of the interview, however, invests the subject with a substantial repertoire of interpretive methods and stock of experiential materials. The active view eschews the image of the vessel waiting to be tapped in favor of the notion that the subject's interpretive capabilities must be activated, stimulated, and cultivated. The interview is a commonly recognized occasion for formally and systematically doing so.

This is not to say that active interviewers merely coax their respondents into preferred responses to their questions. Rather, they converse with respondents in such a way that alternate considerations are brought into play. They may suggest orientations to, and linkages between, diverse aspects of respondents' experience, adumbrating—even inviting—interpretations that make use of particular resources, connections, and outlooks. Interviewers may explore incompletely articulated aspects of experience, encouraging respondents to develop topics in ways relevant to their own experience (DeVault, 1990). The objective is not to dictate interpretation but to provide an environment conducive to the production of the range and complexity of meanings that address relevant issues, and not be confined by predetermined agendas.

Pool's dramaturgic metaphor is apt because it conveys both the structuring conditions and the artfulness of the interview. As a drama of sorts, its narrative is scripted in that it has a topic or topics, distinguishable roles, and a format for conversation. But it also has a developing plot, in which topics, roles, and format are fashioned in the give-and-take of the interview. This active interview is a kind of limited "improvisational" performance. The production is spontaneous, yet structured—focused within loose parameters provided by the interviewer.

Although naturally occurring talk and interaction certainly appear to be more spontaneous, less "staged" than an interview, this is true only in the sense that such interaction is staged by persons other than an interviewer. Resulting conversations are not necessarily more "realis-

18

tic" or "authentic." They simply take place in what have been recognized as indigenous settings. With the development of the interview society, and the increasing deprivatization of personal experience (see Gubrium & Holstein, 1995; Gubrium, Holstein, & Buckholdt, 1994), we find the interview becoming more and more commonplace; interviewing is increasingly becoming a naturally occurring occasion for articulating experience—an experience that increasingly happens to everyone all the time.

Nevertheless, talk about some topics, although being deeply significant, may nonetheless be relatively rare in the normal course of everyday life, even in the interview society. For example, as seemingly ubiquitous as is talk about family and domestic life, we have found it useful to study "family discourse" in a relatively circumscribed range of settings, most of which intentionally provoke talk about family as an integral part of conducting routine business, such as in a family therapy agency, for example (see Gubrium, 1992; Gubrium & Holstein, 1990). Active interviews can thus be used to gain purchase on interpretive practice relating to matters that may not be casually topical. By inciting narrative production, the interviewer may provoke interpretive developments that might emerge too rarely to be effectively captured "in their natural habitat," so to speak.

From a conventional perspective, the active approach to interviewing might seem to invite unacceptable forms of bias. This criticism only holds, however, if one assumes a vastly restricted view of interpretive practice. Bias is a meaningful concept only if the subject is seen to possess a preformed, pure informational commodity that the interview process might somehow contaminate. But if interview responses are seen as products of interpretive practice, they are neither preformed, nor ever pure. They are practical productions. Any interview situation—no matter how formalized, restricted, or standardized—relies on the interaction between interview participants. Because socially constructed meaning is unavoidably collaborative (Garfinkel, 1967; Sacks, Schegloff, & Jefferson, 1974), it is virtually impossible to free any interaction from those factors that could be construed as contaminants. All participants in an interview are inevitably implicated in making meaning.

3. ASSIGNED COMPETENCE AND RESPONDENT SELECTION

Where does the meaning-making process begin? It would seem to start with us, with how we, as researchers, choose to orient to the interview process. If we take either of the conventional approaches, the subjects behind interview participants—both respondent and interviewer—are treated as interpretively passive. They are not taken to be meaning constructors. If, however, we imagine more active subjects, we take account of their "competence" not only as "askers" and "tellers" of experience but also as organizers of the meanings they convey.

Extending this argument, we might ask whom, among all potential meaning-makers, do we select to be actively interviewed and be heard as interpretively competent voices for their experiences? This again implicates the researcher. From a conventional standpoint, competence is understood as a personal quality or trait that individuals either possess or lack. The active approach, however, reframes the concept, treating it as a label that is interactionally applied to persons (Gubrium et al., 1994). Typically, in everyday interaction, attributions of competence can accountably be offered when it can be argued that an individual is able to achieve the communicative goals of a social encounter. But such attributions generally go unexamined, without regard for their social mechanics or to their grounding in interpretive categories that we take for granted, yet employ all the time.

Words of reference can implicitly assign or withhold competence. These labels affect the way we listen to others, leading us to treat some very seriously and to dismiss others as incapable of telling us anything worthwhile. Someone said that to "always talk gibberish," for instance, is not likely to be treated as a source of useful information and probably will be ignored. In formal information gathering, such as police interrogations or personnel background checks, persons assigned to particular categories—ex-convicts, personal friends, or relatives, for example—are considered unreliable sources of information and may not even be consulted. Ideas and decisions about the usefulness of communications are thus mediated by definitions of personal competence, conferring subjective utility, so to speak.

The word *child* commonly operates in this way to affect how one reacts to another's opinions. For example, a mother, participating in a parent effectiveness class, reported the following incident, describing how she "handled it." The mother, otherwise occupied one afternoon, overheard her 5-year-old tell his older sister that she had big pimples and was ugly. The sister responded angrily, yelling at her brother, roughly pushing him aside as she stomped out of his room. The boy burst into tears, repeating what he had said. A loud and hateful argument developed, echoing through the hall, brother and sister shouting from different rooms. The mother walked into her son's room and reprimanded him for teasing his sister. He halfheartedly defended himself, then calmed down, letting the argument die for the time being.

Looking in on her daughter, the mother asked her what happened, comforting her in the process. Through tears and with a choking voice, the daughter repeated what her brother had said, adding bitterly, "He always says things like that and I hate him!" The mother then tried to explain:

Sweetie, he's only a child and doesn't really know what he's saying. Try to remember that, okay? Little kids say all kinds of things like that and if we seriously listened to them, we'd be forever having hurt feelings. Just ignore him. He doesn't know what he's saying and, if he did, he wouldn't be saying it. You're a big girl and big girls know better, don't they?

In effect, the mother was telling her daughter to discount the son's words; as a child, "He doesn't really know what he's saying." He should therefore be ignored. At the same time, the mother implied that if the boy were older, and presumably not a child, he would speak differently and would warrant serious attention. An important distinction was being made here between what was said, on the one hand, and who said it, on the other. The mother urged the daughter to make a particular kind of sense out of the son's words because of the kind of person he was—a child.

This is a quite ordinary way to employ the category "child." Other labels are similarly used to signify competence and incompetence. The other end of the life course, for example, provides words and usages such as "elderly" and "senile," which can suggest that those to whom they are applied cannot competently convey what they think or how they feel and, by implication, cannot be useful respondents.

Assigned Competence in Social Research

How social researchers select those to whom they eventually listen is similarly linked to the assignment of competence. Consider competence as a matter of narration—the ability to tell one's story—in relation to interview respondent selection. The question is, do conceptions of respondent competence unwittingly restrict inquiry into the *hows* and especially the *whats* of the interview process?

In survey research, respondent selection is principally addressed in terms of representativeness, that is, how well the characteristics of those sampled represent the characteristics of the population of interest. One would expect that what is said by a representative sample of respondents in interviews would reflect what the population at large would say if all members were interviewed. The actual process of sample selection, of course, is complex, wending its way among diverse practical contingencies, from cost considerations to physically locating respondents. But the principle of representativeness is paramount.

Researchers typically do not scrutinize the competence assumptions surrounding the words they use to define the population in the first place. In the survey research literature, questions of representativeness are limited to the relationship between sampling elements and the sampling frame. Yet the question of how populations represent people— active subjects—is equally significant and bears directly on narrative competence. Just as the mother applied the term "child" to designate an "incompetent" speaker, as a way of instructing her daughter to disregard a hateful message, the words used to describe the pool of potential interview respondents can work, unwittingly perhaps, to categorize certain people as narratively incompetent. As a result, their voices and the particular *whats* of their lives will not be heard in interview data. Henry Mayhew's (1861-1862) four-volume report, *London Labour and the London Poor*, provides a historic case in point. Mayhew's study was based on interviews and observations conducted among the poor people of London and aimed to document their living conditions from the point of view of the people themselves. The preface of Volume 1 tells us that, until Mayhew considered the idea that one might listen to the voices of the poor as people, the word *poverty* signaled narrative incompetence. For purposes of information gathering, the poor were considered incapable of telling their own story; someone else had to describe their labor and the conditions of their lives. Mayhew (1861-1862) broke with convention, however, to discover that the poor could, indeed, competently speak of life:

> It surely may be considered curious as being the first attempt to publish the history of a people, from the lips of the people themselves—giving a literal description of their labour, their earnings, their trials, and their sufferings, in their own "unvarnished" language; and to portray the condition of their homes and their families by personal observation of the places, and direct communication with the individuals. (p. iii)

Madge (1965) suggests that the idea of interviewing any people about their lives, let alone the poor, was unprecedented at this time, even though the poor and poverty were topics of considerable public debate. Indeed, the word *interview* does not even appear until about the time of Mayhew's study. Although Mayhew was a journalist, the notion of interviewing as a means of gathering facts of experience in general, not to mention the experience of urban poverty, set a precedent for social research, establishing a broad spectrum of persons as narratively competent. The emerging view was that all kinds of people, not just the educated or well-heeled, were competent to give credible voice to experience.

We find a parallel example in the history of psychological research relating to the word *subject*. Tracing the origins of the psychological research subject, Kurt Danziger (1990) compares the social structure of experimentation in three 19th-century laboratories: William Wundt's in Leipzig, Germany; Alfred Binet's in Paris, France; and Francis Galton's in London, England. The disciplinary practices associated with the subject in Wundt's laboratory were distinct from those operating in Binet's and Galton's. Wundt's laboratory privileged "professional" over "lay" subjects in experimentation. The subject was thought to be someone who knew how to respond efficiently and informatively as well as being the target of experimental stimuli. There was a sense in Wundt's laboratory that experimenters knew better than others how to be subjects. Wundt and his students conducted psychophysical experiments, including studies of the psychological experience of "just noticeable differences" between objects placed at various distances from each other on the skin. It was common for the experimenters to act as subjects in these experiments, because it was thought that experimenters could most tellingly identify just what the differences were. Danziger (1990) explains:

> The roles of subject and experimenter were not rigidly segregated, so that the same person could occupy both at different times. Their differentiation was regarded as a matter of practical convenience, and most participants in the laboratory situation could play either or both roles equally well. (p. 51)

The interchangeability of laboratory roles was absent from Binet's and Galton's laboratories.

This historical difference in how the laboratory subject was constituted indicates the important role that words play in guiding courses of action. Danziger notes that the first consistent usage of the term *subject* in experimental psychology was in the context of Binet's clinical experiments. The term acquired further medical connotation in England. The interchangeability of experimental roles in the Leipzig laboratory rested on the belief that nonexperimenters were not as narratively competent as experimenters to report results. The French and English laboratory experience, in contrast, gave greater and more consistent voice to the naive subject, distinguishing this voice from the experimenter's. How experimenters in the respective laboratories selected those to whom they eventually listened (or observed) was linked with presumptions of narrative competence.

A related development in ethnography presents a more recent example. In ethnography, the common term of reference for those who provide researchers with information about their cultures is *informant*. Traditionally, informants were selected on the basis of a rather restricted view of narrative competence. Informants could tell about aspects of their cultures, but they were not asked to interpret what they described. Interpretation and the public presentation of findings in writing were left to the ethnographer. The term *informant* affirmed a rather strict distinction between members of the culture, on the one side, and students of culture and authors of ethnographies, on the other. It was taken for granted that members of a culture could offer little insight into cultural meanings; there was little or no idea that members might have authoritative stories of culture of their own to tell, in their own words and style (cf. Behar, 1993; Burgos-Debray, 1984).

What has come to be called "new ethnography" (Clifford, 1992; Clifford & Marcus, 1986; Gubrium & Holstein, 1995; Marcus & Fischer,

24

1986; Rabinow, 1977) centers in part on a transformation in the idea of narrative competence as it applies to informants. New ethnography takes into account cultural members' own active representations of their worlds, attending closely to the relation between members' and ethnographers' interpretations (Atkinson, 1990; Clough, 1992; Geertz, 1988; Van Maanen, 1988). The leading question in this regard is how cultural members' narrative competence relates to the narrative competence of ethnographers. What is new is the sense that cultural members are coming to be seen as ethnographers in their own right. The term *informant* no longer conveys a distinct difference in narrative competence; instead it signals more of a difference in point of view (Clifford & Marcus, 1986). What seemed at one time to be a division of labor between informant and ethnographer now appears to have been an invidious distinction.

Feminist scholars, perhaps more than anyone, have attempted to explore the ramifications of narrative competence attributions (DeVault, 1990; Fonow & Cook, 1991; Reinharz, 1992; Smith, 1987; Stanley, 1983; Thorne, 1993). Although feminism is theoretically and methodologically diverse, a common concern has been how gender as a cultural and practical set of categories is narratively articulated in society at large and, in particular, in the social and behavioral sciences (Harding, 1987; Thorne, Kramarae, & Henley, 1983). In exploring how women are made invisible as subjects of their own lives and experiences, feminist studies subject traditional assignments of narrative competence to close examination.

Some scholars, like Carol Gilligan (1982), argue that psychological theory has framed the description and evaluation of women's moral experience in hierarchical, individualized, and rationalized—that is, masculine—terms. Relational qualities, said to typify women's development, are suppressed in this framework, effectively silencing women's voices and the particular *whats* of their experience. Others, such as Dorothy Smith (1987, 1990) argue that narrative competence assignments are conditioned by hegemonic institutional and textual practices. In Smith's view, women's experiences, day in and day out, are appropriated more or less silently to the descriptive categories and related practical demands of a world organized in terms of men's working and leisure lives. Smith maintains that if women's experiences are to be represented in terms of where women stand in the world, that standpoint must be a point of departure for analysis. Couching women's experiences in terms derived from other gendered, institutional vocabularies effectively denies women's own lived experience.

Each of these examples illustrates in its own way how assignments of narrative competence work to specify populations worthy of researchers' attention. The issue of who should be selected to speak in interviews appears to precede the question of sample representativeness, going to the very heart of what we mean by people, as opposed to populations. Although studies of urban poverty before Mayhew were ostensibly about the poor population, Mayhew's interviews and observations alerted the 19th-century reader to the possibility that the poor had hardly been heard as people, as narrators of their own lives. Most recently, feminist scholars caution us about the same selection issue, which has operated to exclude the voices of women as people from research populations. The words by which we refer to ourselves and others still have a way of affecting our choice of those to whom we allocate a voice in research.

Guidelines for Active Respondent Selection

The premise that interviewing aims to incite narrative production suggests a general orientation to respondent selection, one that precedes the traditional concern for the representativeness of a sample. Highlighting the interpretively active subject, we must consciously be aware from the start that the selection of interview respondents represents an orientation to people as much as it is the sampling of a population (Willis, 1990, p. 5). The researcher, who, perhaps along with others, will eventually conduct active interviews, must consider the question of people representation while maintaining the more traditional concern for sample representativness.

How is this done in practice? First, we must keep in mind that the word *people*, which we use as a collective term of reference for all potentially appropriate respondents, has a distinctly democratic flavor. It extends interpretive privilege to a wide range of voices, assigning narrative competence to all those placed in the category, recognizing their common worth as human beings and, hence, respondents. This is somewhat at odds with strategies of respondent selection that include or ignore persons on the basis of their "cultural competence" (Johnson,

1990). These strategies seek voices that can impart consensual knowledge but tend to exclude those speaking from alternate standpoints, reflecting different realities. Selecting people, as opposed to representatives of populations, suggests that individuals, in principle, are equally worthy despite individual differences and therefore have worthwhile stories to tell. Although this may complicate the description of culture and experience writ large, it enables and encourages representations of diverse and complex experience.

When Mayhew, for example, referred to the poor of London as people, seriously entertaining the idea that they might be invited to speak of poverty, his project activated them as subjects, including them among those who might be consulted for description of experience. In contrast, those considered to be members of a population are, in a manner of speaking, just there, without individual voice. This has prompted feminist scholars to forcefully raise the issue of how social research overlooks the (population) "just-thereness" of women and, especially, the just-thereness of their household labor (Smith, 1987). Marjorie DeVault (1991), for instance, expressly asks how women as household workers constitute family and care as going concerns. DeVault actively "peoples" the household and house work so that, in her research, we hear the constituting female voices of sustenance and domestic order.

Similarly, Emily Abel (1991) peoples the world of caregiving for frail elderly persons, making visible the gendered categories and interpersonal logic of caregiving activities. Describing the experience of caregiving from the perspective of adult daughters, Abel relates how caregivers themselves understand their endeavors, which, in women's experiences, she argues, ineluctably intertwines "caring about" with "caring for." These domains are regularly separated in studies of caregiving. Analyzing interview data, Anne Opie (1994) complicates the sense of the people who women (and men) are as caregivers by illustrating how differences in caring practices between genders cannot be represented in fixed categories. An orientation to both women and men as caregiving people, not just caregiving women or caregiving men, reveals gender categories constituted by complex social processes, crossing sex-specific boundaries. Using narratively fixed categories such as "men" and "women" as criteria for respondent selection can cause researchers to overlook the possibility that both women and men, as people who give care, can position themselves alike in the ways they describe caregiving.

The key question for respondent selection, then, is whose voices will be heard and whose voices silenced if we conceive of people in particular ways? Although methodological, the question is closely tied to theory in that it requires a critical analysis of the categories and vocabularies used to identify potential respondents. We can imagine Mayhew, for example, grappling with these issues as he planned his study of poverty. The extract from the preface, which we cited earlier, is telling. Using the word *people*, Mayhew conveyed a keen interest in "unvarnished" language and for "direct" communication with those to be studied. It was poor people to whom he directed our attention, not simply an existing population—the poor. As if to distinguish people from population, Mayhew set out to actively study those who could give personal voice to experience in order to publish what he called "the history of a people, from the lips of the people themselves."

Selecting active interview respondents requires critically attending to attributions of narrative competence in the language of social research. Inasmuch as the words by which we refer to ourselves and others have a way of affecting those to whom we choose to listen, the right to be heard as interpretively active and narratively productive is at stake. Categories and labels can be exclusionary, research categories in particular. A critical orientation to the distinction between people and populations works in the opposite direction, alerting us to populations that we might properly take into account as people's voices.

Seeking activated respondents is part and parcel of the active approach to interviewing, not separate from it or primarily a theoretical matter. In practice, consciously selecting respondents because they are assumed to be capable of narrative production continually underscores the theoretical commitment to dignifying and studying interpretive practice. Separating one's interest in a particular population from a concern with the people who comprise that population might enhance the technical purity of the sample selection process, but it does not help to answer the question of who—that is, what *people*—our research findings are about.

Narrators of Experience

Who are these narratively activated people? What are they like as respondents? If the subject behind the respondent is not a passive repository of answers, the interviewer cannot simply uncork the vessel,

28

prying open the sluice gates, so to speak. If the subject is not a vault—not a sealed cache of opinions and emotions—the interviewer seems miscast as a "prospector" for what lies buried from plain sight. What supplants these images? Framing the interview as an occasion for narrative production suggests a vision of the respondent as a story-teller of sorts (Bakhtin, 1981; Bruner, 1986; Myerhoff, 1992; Riessman, 1993; Sarbin, 1986; Todorov, 1984). As with any story, however, the narrator is relating experience at a specific time and place, to a distinctive audience, with particular objectives in mind (Bauman, 1986). Pursuing this image of the interview metaphorically, the storyteller is not reading from a fixed text; he or she is improvising, speaking to the interactional and informational challenges of the immediate circumstances.

But the storyteller is not simply "making it up" as he or she goes along, either. The improvisational narrative combines aspects of experience, emotion, opinion, and expectation, connecting disparate parts into a coherent, meaningful whole. The respondent does not just "make things up" as much as he or she inventively, judiciously, and purposefully fashions a story that is "true to life"—faithful to subjectively meaningful experience—even as it is creatively, spontaneously rendered.

Storytellers draw on their audience too. Their accounts are assembled responsively, in something of a give-and-take with listeners, delivering something of what the audience wants to hear as much as recounting that which merely awaits telling (Gubrium & Buckholdt, 1982). Intentionally active interviewing, however, presents an unusually enterprising audience, at least in comparison to the ones encountered by most respondents. Indeed, the interviewer may request quite specific, detailed stories about particular aspects of the storyteller's life. Questions, prompts, comments, and clarifications point respondents to particular topics, inviting distinctive narrative treatments. The interviewer's directions may be as general or vague as "Tell me what you think about . . ." or as demanding and specific as "On a scale of 1 to 10, tell me how satisfied you are with. . . ." Accordingly, responses range from elaborate life histories to one-word answers.

Storytelling is collaborative, but not simply in the conventional sense that interviewers ask questions and respondents provide answers. Rather, the interviewer and respondent interact more dynamically to produce meaningful stories. Where the traditional view of the interview process draws a clear distinction between the tasks and roles of the interviewer and the respondent, the active view of the interview points to a greater range of interpretive activities of both parties. Of course the interviewer asks questions, but so might the respondent. The interviewer suggests topics of interest and appropriate ways of addressing the topics. But the interviewer's questions and prompts are not mere stimuli, catalysts for the reflexlike production of answers. They are more like framing devices that the respondent might follow in characterizing experience, interpretive incitements and themes for storytelling. At the same time, the respondent pursues his or her own story lines, as it were, both appraising and inquiring into the interpretive possibilities that are available for addressing the narrative demands of the interview.

Challenged by the interviewer, pointed in promising directions, and at least partially aware of the interpretive terrain at hand, the respondent becomes a kind of researcher in his or her own right, consulting repertoires of experience and orientations, linking fragments into patterns, and offering "theoretically" coherent descriptions, accounts, and explanations. Far from merely reporting a chronicle of what is already present (hidden or obscured as it might be), the respondent actively composes meaning by way of situated, assisted inquiry.

The interviewer is far from irrelevant to this project, but his or her contributions are not so specified or determinant as in the traditional interview model. The interviewer invites and assists narrative production, suggesting the parameters of the sort of narrative being solicited. The active interview is not so much dictated by a predesigned set of specific questions as it is loosely directed and constrained by the interviewer's topical agenda, objectives, and queries. The image is more of a storyteller on a rather slack interpretive tether to the interviewer's project, not a respondent tightly anchored to an interview schedule. In principle, this storyteller is all people, in their capacities as competent narrators of their lives.

4. NARRATIVE RESOURCES

What fund of experiential knowledge does the storytelling respondent summon to formulate his or her narratives? How does the respondent use this repository? Let us compare two kinds of answers to these questions.

One answer, of course, derives from the notion that the fund of knowledge is a vessel of answers and that access is relatively straightforward. In this view, the respondent ideally reports concisely and accurately his or her subjective sentiments, feelings, and behaviors. The respondent acts as the *reporter* of the subject's knowledge. The other kind of answer stems from the view that the fund of knowledge is a diverse, multifaceted, and emerging resource and that access to it is actively selective and constructive. In this view, the respondent both construes and calls on what is considered relevant in relation to the matters under consideration in the interview, assembling the information so that it makes sense as a response, that it coalesces into a circumstantially sensible and relevant story. In this case, the respondent acts as the *narrator* of experiential knowledge.

Constructing the Stock of Knowledge

Viewing the respondent as narrator, the active approach features a subject possessing a fund or *stock* of knowledge that is simultaneously substantive, reflexive, and emergent (Schütz, 1967). In practice, that which relevantly comprises the respondent's stock of knowledge depends on how parties to the interview construe and manage their respective roles in relation to what is being asked about and the answers being conveyed. What the respondent accesses in her stock of knowledge depends on the role she takes, on whether, say, she is speaking as a mother, as an adult daughter, or as a spouse. As Pool (1957) implied earlier, the experiential information or data obtained in the interview are as much about the particular drama from which that information or data are obtained as about the respondent's experience. Quite apart from the ostensible neutrality of the interview and the unbiased interviewer, the respondent's stock of knowledge can shift about in the course of the interview in relation to the role taken by the respondent. (This applies to the interviewer as well and will be discussed in Chapters 5 and 6.) For all practical purposes, the stock of knowledge is always the stock at hand.

Take a respondent who describes the home care she provides for her aged mother with dementia. When the respondent speaks as an adult daughter, her vessel of answers, as it were, might be very different from when she speaks as a spouse (see Abel, 1991). Speaking as an adult daughter, the respondent is likely to frame her answer in terms of the events and sentiments of the daughter and mother's interpersonal history. Speaking as a spouse, the experiential purview of the respondent's answers keys into relations with her husband and their domestic affairs. Further complications arise when it is not clear what position she takes in responding to interview items. The stock of knowledge is emergent in the sense that the respondent not only conveys information about his or her life but simultaneously activates and manages—narrates—what is accessed and the diverse meanings that this entails.

The narrating respondent's stock of knowledge is quite different from the passive respondent's vessel of answers. As a narrative resource, the stock of knowledge might be likened to several different shifting vessels of answers. In this regard, the vessels that are "there" and available for securing and conveying answers depend on the role or situated identity of the respondent. What is evidently there when the respondent, say, speaks as an adult daughter is not necessarily what is evidently there when she speaks as a spouse, a mother, or someone else. The circumstantial "thereness" or practical substance of this respondent's stock of knowledge depends on the position she takes in reaching back into her experience, retrieving information, and formulating an answer.

The analogy of the multiple, shifting vessels of answers does not fully capture the dynamic features of narrative resources, however. For example, the respondent who speaks of caregiving from the point of view of the adult daughter may, in the course of the interview, for the very first time admittedly consider what she might feel about her mother from the perspective of being her husband's wife. The ostensible vessel of answers from which she retrieves her answers in this instance substantively emerges *within* the interview, as the respondent considers how she might answer questions from that point of view. Strictly speaking, the analogy is not only a matter of shifting vessels but the simultaneous production of new vessels. The complex contents of the respondent's stock of knowledge are intertwined with the identities partaking in the interview.

Stocks of knowledge are only partially historical. Because the knowledge the respondent calls on is always knowledge-in-the-making, it does not purely reflect the respondent's past. The past is linked with what is being made of the present, that is, the respective positions from which one can speak of life. In the preceding example, the respondent's history cannot directly convey the caregiving experience. What is conveyed—its experiential details and progress over time—depends on what is being made of the present—the role one takes—in the interview. As Michel Foucault (1979, p. 31) might put it, the history of the active respondent's experience is a history of the present. For the "same" respondent, we can imagine that there might be an adult daughter's version of caregiving, with its past attitudes and feelings; a spouse's version, with its particular history of sentiments; and so on. Putting this form of history in dramatic terms, we might say that each present role tells the story of its own past attitudes, feelings, and behaviors.

The active respondent constructs his or her experiential history as the interview unfolds, in collaboration with the active interviewer. The respondent's history is a history-in-the-making, complexly unfolding in relation to what has taken place in the past, to what is currently being made of the past, and to immediate prospects for the future. Whether experience is elicited in the form of opinions, feelings, or behaviors, it is as much a feature of the present as of the past. An opinion, for example, about the past cognitive status of one's mother is an opinion elicited and conveyed in terms of the particular perspective on the past being taken by the respondent. There are, then, several opinions about the mother's past cognitive status, depending on whether one's story is being told, say, from the perspective of an adult daughter, wife, or working mother. Indeed, there is no reason to limit narrative resources to these particular perspectives, as the respondent may take any viewpoint that he or she considers empirically warrantable.

What we, as researchers, make of the respondent who says that she feels both hateful and "totally loving" toward her mother depends on how we construe the respondent's relation to her fund of experiential knowledge. Viewing the respondent as a mere reporter of what lies in a vessel of answers suggests that we are getting a contradiction and that we must probe for the respondent's true or actual thoughts or feelings. Viewing the respondent as narratively active, however, suggests that the variability and contradictions of the experience under consideration be examined in relation to the interview's interpretive circumstances. In the active approach, it would be normal and routine for the respondent to offer complex descriptions of experience because, at the very least, the respondent's stock of knowledge avails her of varied funds of information, and the active respondent has a continuing hand in the variability.

What the active respondent says is as much constructed as it is tapped from narrative resources. The respondent's stock of knowledge grows, diminishes, and is altered as the interview develops. As a narrative resource, the stock of knowledge may even be inadvertently deconstructed, such as when the ordinary yet savvy respondent, looking back on what she said at the start of an interview, comments that all the evident contradictions in her responses are "really" matters of "how you look at things," products of the perspective one takes.

Judith Globerman, a colleague at the University of Toronto, shared a vivid illustration of the transformation of respondents' stocks of knowledge from her interviews with caregivers of people with dementia. A year after caregivers were first interviewed, a second round of interviews showed that respondents recalled in detail what they had said in earlier interviews. More to the point, the respondents commented on their earlier responses, considering the earlier opinions, feelings, and actions in relation to what they now thought and felt. The comments indicated that what seemed in the initial interviews to have been straightforward and consistent reports were transformed in quality, not just in degree, when the respondent was given a second opportunity to "think about it."

Positional Shifts and Resource Activation

Access to the narrative resources we have called stocks of knowledge does not operate in the passive way that access to the vessels of answers does. The simultaneous substantive, reflexive, and emergent features of stocks of knowledge require a more dynamic approach. With the interviewer's help, the respondent *activates* different aspects of his or her stock of knowledge, which we can hear in the conversational give-and-take of the interview. In the course of many open-ended interviews, for example, respondents intersperse their responses to interview items with telltale phrases such as "speaking as a mother," "thinking like a woman," "if I were in her shoes," "after I heard what he said," "wearing my professional hat," "on second thought," "when you bother to think about it," "now that you ask," "I'm not sure about that one," and "I haven't really thought about it." The phrases tell of changing roles, shifts in narrative positions that, in turn, signal stocks of knowledge pertinent to the point of view being taken or the complexities of telling. Positions may shift several times in the course of an interview. At one point, it may be clear that the respondent is speaking as an adult daughter; at another point, she evidently takes the role of a spouse. Or it may not be evident whose point of view is being taken, in which case the active interviewer is both analytically and procedurally obliged to seek clarification (see Chapters 5 and 8). At some point, a new role and perspective may be prompted by the interview questions themselves, such as when the respondent admits that he or she had not thought about the matter under consideration before and unknowingly proceeds to do just that as the interview continues. Indeed, occasionally, the respondent's comments may suggest that the point of view he or she takes is that of the "respondent," a role the respondent subsequently admits as having never taken before. For example, when a respondent becomes visibly anxious after a tape recorder is turned on and states that she does not know if she can think clearly with "that thing" on, we might infer that what will be said with the recorder turned on might not align with what would otherwise be said. The vessel-of-answers approach would necessarily take this to be a matter of reactivity. For the active respondent, however, it signals alternative validities, whose distinctive narrative resources *naturally* (and validly) convey equally acceptable responses.

To illustrate the multiplicity of positions and perspectives that respondents may take, consider the following extract from an open-ended interview with an adult daughter who cared for her mother, who had dementia, at home. The daughter was employed part-time and shared the household with her employed husband and their two sons, one a part-time college student and the other a full-time security guard. The extract begins when the interviewer (I) asked the adult daughter (R) to describe her feelings about having to juggle so many needs and schedules. This related to a discussion of the so-called sandwich generation, which was said to be caught between having to raise families and seeing to the needs of frail elderly parents. Note how, after the interviewer asked the respondent what she meant by saying that she had mixed feelings, the respondent made explicit reference to various ways of thinking about the matter, as if to suggest that more than one narrative resource (with contradictory responses) might be brought to bear on the matter. The respondent displayed considerable narrative activity: She not only referenced possible *whats* of caregiving and family life but, in the process, informed the interviewer of *how* she could construct her answer.

I: We were talking about, you said you were a member of the, what did you call it?

R: They say that I'm in the sandwich generation. You know, like we're sandwiched between having to care for my mother . . . and my grown kids and my husband. People are living longer now and you've got different generations at home and, I tell ya, it's a mixed blessing.

I: How do you feel about it in your situation?

R: Oh, I don't know. Sometimes I think I'm being a bit selfish because I gripe about having to keep an eye on Mother all the time. If you let down your guard, she wanders off into the backyard or goes out the door and down the street. That's no fun when your hubby wants your attention too. Norm works the second shift and he's home during the day a lot. I manage to get in a few hours of work, but he doesn't like it. I have pretty mixed feelings about it.

I: What do you mean?

R: Well, I'd say that as a daughter, I feel pretty guilty about how I feel sometimes. It can get pretty bad, like wishing that Mother were just gone, you know what I mean? She's been a wonderful mother and I love her very much, but if you ask me how I feel as a wife and mother, that's another matter. I feel like she's [the mother], well, intruding on our lives and just making hell out of raising a family. Sometimes I put myself in my husband's shoes and I just know how he feels. He doesn't say much, but I know that he misses my company, and I miss his of course. [Pause] So how do you answer that?

The interviewer then explained that the respondent could answer in the way she believed best represented her thoughts and feelings. But as the exchange unfolded, it was evident that "best" misrepresented the narrative complexity of the respondent's thoughts and feelings. In the following extract, notice how the respondent struggled to sort her responses to accord with categorically distinct identities. At one point, she explained that she now knew how a wife could and should feel because she gathered from the way her husband and sons acted that "men don't feel things in the same way." This suggested that her own thoughts and feelings were constructively derived from a fund of gendered knowledge as well. Note, too, how at several points, the interviewer collaborated with the respondent to define her identity as a respondent. At the very end of the extract, the respondent suggested that other respondents' answers might serve to clarify the way she herself organized her responses.

R: I try to put myself in their [husband's and sons'] shoes, try to look at it from their point of view, you know, from a man's way of thinking. I ask myself how it feels to have a part-time wife and mama. I ask myself how I'd feel. Believe me, I know he [husband] feels pretty rotten about it. Men get that way; they want what they want and the rest of the time, well, they're quiet, like nothing's the matter. I used to think I was going crazy with all the stuff on my mind and having to think about everything all at once and not being able to finish with one thing and get on to the other. You know how it gets—doing one thing and feeling bad about how you did something else and wanting to redo what you did or what you said. The way a woman does, I guess. I think I've learned that about myself. I don't know. It's pretty complicated thinking about it. [Pause] Let's see, how do I really feel?

I: Well, I was just wondering, you mentioned being sandwiched earlier and what a woman feels?

R: Yeah, I guess I wasn't all that sure what women like me feel until I figured out how Norm and the boys felt. I figured pretty quick that men are pretty good at sorting things out and that, well, I just couldn't do it, 'cause, well, men don't feel things the same way. I just wouldn't want to do that way anyway. Wouldn't feel right about it as a woman, you know what I mean? So, like they say, live and let live, I guess.

I: But as a daughter?

R: Yeah, that too. So if you ask me how I feel having Mother underfoot all the time, I'd say that I remember not so far back that I was underfoot a lot when I was a little girl and Mother never complained, and she'd help Dad out in the store too. So I guess I could tell you that I'm glad I'm healthy and around to take care of her and, honestly, I'd do it all over again if I had to. I don't know. You've talked to other women about it. What do they say?

I: Well, uh.

R: Naw, I don't want to put you on the spot. I was just thinking that maybe if I knew how others in my shoes felt, I might be able to sort things out better than I did for ya.

Such comments about both the subject matter under consideration and how one does or should formulate responses are far too common in interviews to ignore. They show that the respondent, in collaboration with the interviewer, activates narrative resources as an integral part of exchanging questions and answers. Yet, because the activation process is not considered to be a proper part of standardized interviewing, it is not taken into account as data. A possible exception is the place traditionally left at the end of interview schedules for interviewer remarks. Ironically, Converse and Schuman (1974) admit in *Conversations at Random* that "survey research as interviewers see it" is replete with activation. One might take this as an implicit concession: If interviewers' accounts were taken seriously, interviews and interview data would be testaments to interpretive activity. But faithful and guarded professional adherence to the vessel-of-answers view belies it.

Treating the interview as active allows the interviewer to encourage the respondent to shift positions in the interview so as to explore alternate perspectives and stocks of knowledge. Rather than searching for the best or most authentic answer, the aim is to systematically activate applicable ways of knowing—the possible answers—that respondents can reveal, as diverse and contradictory as they might be. This, of course, implicates an active interviewer, to whom we now turn.

5. THE ACTIVE INTERVIEWER

Even survey research methodology holds that interviewers must be active, but within fairly strict limits. Interviewers are instructed to skillfully solicit answers, but to preformulated questions, under constraints designed to keep them from contaminating that which lies within the passive respondent's vessel of answers. Indeed, restraint may be the byword of standardized interviewing, as interviewers are typically admonished to follow guidelines like the following:

1. Read the questions exactly as worded.
2. If the respondent's answer to the initial question is not a complete and adequate answer, probe for clarification and elaboration in a way that does not influence the content of the answers that result.
3. Answers should be recorded without interviewer discretion; the answers recorded should reflect what the respondent says, and they should only reflect what the respondent says.
4. The interviewer communicates a neutral, nonjudgmental stance with respect to the substance of the answers. The interviewer should not provide any personal information that might imply any particular values or preference with respect to topics covered in the interview, nor should the interviewer provide any feedback to respondents, positive or negative, with respect to the specific content of the answers they provide. (Fowler & Mangione, 1990, p. 33)

This image of the interviewer as a disinterested catalyst seems at odds with interviewing practice. Although interviewers are told to "merely soak up information like a sponge, without giving any back" (Backstrom & Hursh, 1963, p. 135), Converse and Schuman (1974) also tell us that interviewers face the "continuing cross pressures" of conducting neutral inquiry within the context of a conversation (pp. 22-36). Attempts to remain uninvolved typically fail. Indeed, research suggests that as much as 50% of everything interviewers say after a survey interview begins is something other than a designed question or a neutral probe (Cannell, Fisher, & Marquis, 1968). The conversation is not merely incidental "chatter," but involves talk that is central to doing the research.

Activating Narrative Production

If interviewers are as deeply implicated in the production of responses as this suggests, we need to consider an alternative conceptualization of the interviewer's role. Although the respondent actively constructs and assembles answers, he or she does not simply "break out" talking, so to speak. Neither elaborate narratives nor one-word replies leap from the respondent without provocation. The active interviewer is responsible for inciting respondents' answers. But the active interviewer does far more than dispassionate questioning; he or she *activates narrative production*. Where the standardized approach attempts to strip the interview of all but the most neutral, impersonal stimuli, the consciously active interviewer intentionally, concertedly provokes responses by indicating—even suggesting—narrative positions, resources, orientations, and precedents for the respondent to engage in addressing the research questions under consideration.

The active interviewer sets the general parameters for responses, constraining as well as provoking answers that are germane to the researcher's interest. He or she does not tell respondents what to say, but offers them pertinent ways of conceptualizing issues and making connections, pertinence being partly defined by the research topic and partly by the substantive horizons of ongoing responses. The active respondent may selectively exploit a vast range of narrative resources, but it is the active interviewer's job to direct and harness the respondent's constructive storytelling to the research task at hand.

Incitement and Narrative Precedence

Preformulated questions may serve as catalysts for respondents' answers, but myriad other interactional and discursive gestures also provoke and shape responses. The mere invitation to participate in an interview, for example, is sometimes more than sufficient incitement for some respondents. Consider how little it took to provoke an extended, detailed life story during a study of elderly residents of adult congregate-living facilities, for example. In this case, the interviewer (I) introduced himself to the respondent, briefly explained the purpose of the interview, then launched his inquiry with the briefest of requests. The respondent (R) replied enthusiastically.

I: Tell me about your life.

R: Well, because of this older brother, I had such empathy for him that it really handicapped my life briefly. He was not invited to parties and I was and because of him, I wouldn't go and so this colored my life as I grew up. . . .

Thirty minutes later, the respondent was still in the midst of the story. Finally, following the respondent's comment about his "punchiness," the interviewer asked his first question:

R: . . . I feel like a prize fighter who's been in the ring too long, and I'm a little punchy right now.

I: If you were to write the story of your life, let's say, what would the chapters be about?

With the exception of some minor displays of attentiveness, and a few brief requests for clarification, the interviewer had not intervened in a half-hour narrative, a story comprising accounts of life, love, hardship, work, occupation, family, and other unanticipatable concerns of the moment. The respondent needed little prompting to activate his narrative proclivities. It seemed that the "interview" was hardly necessary.

Still, our preceding descriptions of the interview situation tended to gloss over what proved to be several important ways that the interviewer provided narrative incitement and precedence for the emerging life history. We noted above, for example, that "the interviewer introduced himself to the respondent, briefly explained the purpose of the interview, then launched his inquiry with the briefest of requests," mentioning this merely "in passing," as if it were incidental to the information-gathering process. But we neglected to show how important this "preliminary" work is for evoking the respondent's story.

From the active perspective, all aspects of interviewer-respondent interaction can provide precedents for how to proceed. Starting with the very introduction of the interviewer and the study itself, the interviewer offers resources and points of reference for the conversation to come. In the example above, respondents were told that a researcher from the university would like to talk to them about their lives and experiences, right up to the present. Each interview began the same way: "Everyone has a life story. Tell me about your life, in about 20 minutes or so if you can. Begin with whatever you'd like." Regardless of how brief or innocuous, this introduction of the study topic and the initial invitation to speak served to inform respondents that important "researchers" were interested in respondents' stories. Moreover, the introduction focused on the respondent's life *as a whole* in relation to current circumstances, no matter how trivial or mundane the respondent might think that experience was. The emerging life story then provided an emerging empirical basis for inviting respondents to talk further about aspects of their past, present, and future that might be relevant to the study.

Even the mere identity of the researcher primed respondent's stories, positioning respondents in relation to how they might respond. Simply having the opportunity to have a college professor or an "expert in the field" ask for one's opinion was incentive enough for many respondents to construct marvelously detailed life histories. By the same token, some respondents are inhibited by the "importance" of authority figures. Similarly, an older female respondent might orient to a younger interviewer "as a mother" if the interviewer did not encourage an alternate understanding of their relationship. Or a respondent might assume the role of "the expert" if the interviewer was able to present him- or herself as ignorant or curious about the subject at hand, not an expert in his or her own right. The point is not that particular identity framings are preferable for establishing good rapport or maintaining an unbiased atmosphere. Rather, it is that the presentation of *any* identity is an activity that must be considered and can, to a degree, be actively manipulated to facilitate talk about relevant subject matters. This is not something to be eliminated or standardized; it is something to be actively used to productively engage respondents in the research task.

Conditioning Stories

Like interviewer identity, talk that is conventionally seen to *merely* introduce a study, smooth out conversation, or cultivate rapport can also be viewed as an active, consequential part of the interviewing process. In the standard model, such talk is considered incidental to the collection of information, done only to facilitate communication. Understood in this way, introductory remarks and statements made to ease transitions from one question to another are designed with an eye toward their neutrality. But in the active interview, we can see how such talk clearly provides precedence and direction.

The introduction to an interview is something of a signpost to guide active respondents through the open terrain of their experience. It can suggest relevant ways of thinking about and linking experience, bringing alternate resources into play, conditioning the stories that emerge. Consider how the following three introductions to standardized interview studies provide distinctive precedence for respondent participation.

Introduction A

Hello! I'm _____ from the National Opinion Research Center. We're conducting a national survey about how people are feeling in general about the kinds of activities people do in their leisure time—that is, their spare time when they are not working. There are questions about your moods, and about the time you spend watching television or going to sports events, about your social activities, and some about your use of alcoholic drinks. (Sudman & Bradburn, 1983, p. 216)

Introduction B

In the past few years there has been a lot of discussion about what policies and activities of our state colleges and universities should be. Some of the questions being asked here at Washington State University (WSU) include these: is WSU meeting the needs and desires of the state's residents? . . . We are conducting this study because we feel that the residents of Washington, all of whom support WSU through the taxes they pay, should have their opinions heard on these important matters. (Dillman, 1978, p. 168)

Introduction C

As a former student, your school is interested in how well the vocational and non-vocational programs met your needs to make a living. (Dillman, 1978, p. 168)

Designed merely to introduce a standardized interview study, tell what the study was about, and convince the respondent of the study's utility, none of these was seriously considered for the extent to which it conditioned the interview process. In its own way, however, each opening gambit significantly positions the respondent in relation to the questions that are about to be asked. Introduction A, for example, prepares the respondent to engage the interview on a very "ordinary" basis. It seeks the opinion of a respondent who is cast a one of "the people" who have feelings about a number of mundane issues. The introduction stresses how it is "your" opinions, moods, and activities that are important. In contrast, Introduction B positions the respondent as a taxpaying resident of the state who has a right to voice an opinion on how revenues are spent. Introduction C is even more specific in asking for opinions of "former students." Each of these introductions actively designates a distinctive perspective from which the respondent is to respond. Intentional or not, the respondent is placed at a particular vantage point, implicitly, if not expressly, suggesting orientations to the interview topic and the questions to follow.

An activated interviewer can more explicitly take account of such positioning opportunities by specifically and strategically suggesting standpoints. For example, consider what was accomplished during an interview study of interorganizational relations and the coordinating function of a community-based cancer control agency, Community Cancer Control (CCC). The loosely structured interview study was introduced to "key informants" by asking them to discuss and evaluate how well CCC had been able to coordinate the diverse activities of other cancer control organizations in the area. The introduction explicitly told respondents that they "were selected to speak for your organization in evaluating CCC." Responding from this perspective, an executive of a university-based cancer center offered the following response: "CCC can't be thought of in terms of effective coordination. . . . It wasn't coordinated when they walked into an organization right after we did. . . . Sometimes we got in each other's way, competed for the same things." Later, near the end of the interview, the interviewer intentionally asked the executive to reposition herself: "If you think of CCC from the point of view of the Oncology Organizations Coordinating Group [a coalition of top-level executives], how would you evaluate its coordination?" The executive replied, "As much as I saw us duplicating services, I have to admit that getting us together on a regular basis certainly helped us clarify our respective roles, clear our calendars, let us know what we were all thinking, and the like."

The active interviewer thus provoked evaluations using situationally variable criteria, leading to strikingly different assessments. From the vessel-of-answers approach, one would certainly question the reliability of this interview, given the two distinctly different—hence "unreliable"—answers given to ostensibly the same question. But viewing this in terms of active interviewing, by repositioning the respondent, the interviewer was able to elicit two equally legitimate and authoritative evaluations, each reflecting an organizationally circumscribed orientation to different, yet vital, aspects of the situation in question. Nearly every aspect of the interview conversation can condition responses. In standardized interviewing, for example, transition statements are viewed as conversational bridges between questions. They are considered necessary interactional devices, largely incidental to the production of actual answers. But these devices can also invite consequential shifts in orientation that influence respondents' interpretive focus. Consider how the following internal transition between specific survey interview questions urges the respondent to assume a unique interpretive position, a process similar to that seen in the previously discussed introductions.

> Even though it may be very unlikely, think for a moment about how various areas of your life might be different if you were separated (from your spouse). For each of the following areas, how do you think things would change? (Institute for Survey Research, 1987)

Note how the transition maneuvers the respondent into a position from which to answer ensuing questions. Indeed, the statement is a virtual set of instructions, telling the respondent how to think about what to say.

Other "orienting" statements may suggest diverse interpretive resources, even though they intend to legitimize a particular range of responses. The following transition and introduction to a survey question, for example, offers specific alternatives for how a respondent might feel about "the government in Washington," implicitly discouraging other alternatives.

> Some people are afraid the government in Washington is getting too powerful for the good of the country and the individual person. Others feel that the government in Washington is not getting too strong. Do you have an opinion on this or not? (Center for Political Studies, 1992)

Here, the interviewer explicitly provides exemplars of particular opinions, suggesting an appropriate way that the respondent might frame the topic under consideration.

The point is not to criticize these standardized forms for their inadvertent contamination of the respondents' perspectives. Rather, these examples illustrate how active even the most ostensibly passive interview must inevitably be. Recognizing that interpretation is always context dependent, active interviewing can be more explicit in the ways that it manipulates frames of reference for narrative production.

Using Background Knowledge

Sensitivity to context underscores the need for interviewers to be at least minimally aware of the cultural and "ethnographic background" within which interviews are embedded. Interviewers are often cautioned that they must "know the local setting" to ask good questions and interpret the meaning of answers (see Briggs, 1986; Cicourel, 1964). By drawing on background knowledge, active interviewers can make their research more productive, incorporating indigenous interpretive resources, perspectives, and landmarks into their inquiries. This is, of course, an implicit argument in favor of combining ethnographic observation with interviewing, not only to heighten rapport with, and understanding of, informants but to take advantage of, and reveal, the local *whats* of experience.

The interviewer's background knowledge can sometimes be an invaluable resource for assisting respondents to explore and describe their circumstances, actions, and feelings. Indeed, citing shared experience is often a useful way of providing concrete referents on which inquiries and answers can focus. For example, during a study of involuntary commitment proceedings leading to the hospitalization of persons who allegedly were mentally ill (see Holstein, 1993), the researcher conducted several interviews with representatives of the District Attorney's office (DAs), looking for insight into DAs' case management and argumentation strategies. Although informative, most of these interviews yielded responses that portrayed DAs' actions as strictly "by the book." That is, the DAs described what they did and how they handled cases in terms of the ideal model of how involuntary commitment cases should be conducted, offering few details of how daily practice might relate to the model.

Having observed dozens of cases for this study, the researcher became progressively more familiar with everyday courtroom events, and, in the course of one interview with a DA, eventually began to refer to cases he had witnessed over the past few weeks. Instead of asking a rather abstract question like "How do you convince the judge that candidate patients can't function in their daily lives?" the researcher was able to ask, "Yesterday, you got that guy to say several things that seemed to strike everyone as real signs of trouble. How did that happen?" Prompted by several additional questions about specific aspects of the case in question, the DA proceeded to explain in great detail how he worked through the interrogation of this particular candidate patient, at the same time generalizing about his typical interrogation practices in relation to this specific case. Eventually, he concluded by saying, "I was just letting him hang himself," furnishing a colorful vernacular label for one of the practices that became an analytic focus for subsequent analyses of the commitment process (Holstein, 1988, 1993).

The experience of interviewing itself can provide useful background knowledge. The information and sentiments that particular respondents present can serve as the basis for concretely relating to the experience of other respondents. Whereas the standardized interview would try to limit informational "spillage" from one interview to another, active interviewing takes advantage of the growing stockpile of background knowledge that the interviewer collects in prior interviews to pose concrete questions and explore facets of respondents' circumstances that would not otherwise be probed.

Prior experience can thus be used as a resource by both interviewers and respondents. As the interviewer becomes aware of the circumstances of respondents' activities and circumstances, he or she can refer to those circumstances as a way of linking the respondent's experiential location to the researcher's more conceptual issues and questions. Respondents have something to which they might concretely attach their narratives. And both can make sense of the conversation because of their familiarity with the circumstances in question. DeVault (1990) argues that sensitive feminist interviewing requires competent asking and listening grounded in background knowledge of women's experience. We want to generalize her message: Background knowledge in *any* research circumstance, involving *all types* of interviewers and respondents, provides direction and precedent, connecting the researcher's interest to the respondent's experience, bridging the concrete and abstract.

Narrative Guidance and Constraint

Active interviewing is not confined to asking questions and recording answers. Like other instances of ordinary conversation, trouble-free exchanges rely on mutual attentiveness, monitoring, and responsiveness (Sacks et al., 1974). Rather than tightly restricting interviewer participation as the standardized model prescribes, active interviewers may judiciously engage the respondent, working interactionally to establish the discursive bases from which the respondent can articulate his or her relevant experiences. This involves a certain amount of give-and-take that is anathema to standardized procedures. Not only does the interviewer "keep the conversation going," so to speak, but he or she also provides the respondent with a measure of narrative guidance that maintains the necessary research focus.

Consider, for example, the way that interviewers in different "life course" interviews helped formulate and sustain the parameters of emerging life stories, guiding narrative construction in the process. In one study concerned with the quality of life for nursing home residents in relation to life as a whole (see Gubrium, 1993), the research design called for a set of loosely formulated questions intended to elicit a free-flowing story of life events and occurrences that proved important to the elderly subjects. The study emphasized the subjective construction of significant patterns and interpretations of one's life, especially in relation to present concerns. One interview produced the following exchange between the interviewer (I) and an 83-year-old widow (R).

I: A lot of people think of their lives as having had a particular course, as having gone up and down. Some people think it hasn't gone down. Some people see it as having gone in a circle. How do you see your life? Which way has it gone?

R: My life has been a tangle, but with all my troubles, I've had a pretty good life. Been able to take care of myself and [pause] until now [the respondent had recently broken her hip].

I: How has your life been a tangle, would you say?

R: Well, getting there [getting married for the first time] and then separating, and God gave me one good marriage. He was so good to me and so loving! Both of us were up in age.

I: You think that made a difference, that you were up in age?

R: Yeah, I think I would have gotten along better. We didn't have enough money and I was working from 6:00 in the morning to 2:30, maybe longer, and put in extra hours and make all the money I could to help take care of the home.

I: What were you doing?

R: Working in a cafe. . . . I made pretty good money, even back then. You could buy more with a dime back then than you can with a dollar now. Gosh it's terrible now. But I still go on. I still have fun, just going around talking to these people here. . . . I don't like sitting. This wheelchair got my butt paralyzed [R laughs]. But I do get up and walk down with the banisters and walk behind the wheelchair.

I: If you could draw your life on paper?

R: It would be such a tangle you couldn't read it and I couldn't either. I tell you, I've always been happy. I don't know why. Until my son died and my husband died. He died in '73. He was 73 years old and died in '73.

I: Are there any particular things that happened in your life that changed the shape of it, the course of it? The main things, what would you say they were?

R: Well, my oldest son, he was in the army. . . .

The respondent proceeded to elaborate a detailed life story linking mundane family matters, her concerns for her son while he was in the military overseas, her home, her beloved second husband, her career as a waitress, and myriad other details of a life that emerged as a veritable experiential labyrinth, the meaning of which was thoroughly linked to the complicated, meandering pattern established in the story.

Note in this instance how the interviewer offered precedent for thinking of life in terms of a "course" with many possible shapes. In doing so, he staked out loose narrative parameters for the life story he was soliciting, parameters that he gently reasserted at several junctures in the ensuing conversation. At first, he actively guided the respondent in the direction of the "tangle" that she offered as a metaphor for her life, and later edged her story back "on course," that is, refocused the story on the life course by asking her once again to picture "the main things." Although never intrusive, the interviewer nonetheless guided and constrained the respondent's narrative so that it continued to address the general research agenda as the respondent formulated her own story.

Compare this to the life stories elicited in interviews by Douglas Kimmel (1974). Kimmel organized his inquiries around a developmental model of the life course in which life course variation could be traced to "turning points" or "milestones" that alter what might otherwise be fairly predictable patterns of aging. Note the difference in the life story that Kimmel (K) elicited by urging his 27-year-old male respondent (G) to employ the milestone imagery.

K: As you look back over your life, what are some of the milestones that stand out?

G: In terms of just profession, in terms of personal life? Do you want specifics?

K: Yes.

G: What made me choose my profession?

K: Was that a milestone?

G: It certainly was. . . .

K: And that was the turning point for you?

G: I look back and that's what I remember, so that's a milestone for me, what one would have to call a milestone. . . . Anyway, other milestones. Oh, I'm sure I have some. Oh! Telling my folks I was gay was a milestone. . . .

K: What about more recent milestones? Like coming to New York?

G: Well, coming to New York wasn't really a milestone for me because that was so planned, so matter-of-fact that I was going to do it that it wasn't really a milestone. . . .

K: . . . What about crisis points? Have there been any crisis points that stand out?

G: Yes, I've had a lot of crises. Do you want some of them?

K: Yes. . . . Have there been any crisis points in your relationship with your family?

G: Not really. Some childish things. Nothing really recently. I've never run away from my family or anything like that as a child.

K: You said at one point when we didn't have the recorder on that your mother was in the hospital.

G: Yeah, she is.

K: Is this a serious matter?

G: It's not, now, as it's turned out, thank goodness. Oh, I see what you mean, a crisis in those terms. (Kimmel, 1974, pp. 116-120)

Here, the interviewer repeatedly offered the language of milestones, turning points, and crises as a resource for characterizing the respondent's life. Not "putting words in the respondent's mouth" but, rather, making a specific vocabulary salient, and repeatedly asserting its descriptive utility, by the end of this extract, the interviewer had virtually trained the respondent to think and speak of his life in the terms relevant to the research at hand.

Although standardized approaches would focus on the ways that the two interviewers above were apparently contaminating the data that ostensibly resided within their subjects' repositories of knowledge, the active alternative urges us to understand the interviewers contribution quite differently. If one rejects the model of the passive vessel of answers, the notion of contamination is not so compelling. Instead, by conceiving of interviews as ineluctably collaborative, we can recognize how the interviewers shaped these conversations without rejecting the final products as somehow defiled or tainted. These life narratives may be taken to reflect interpretive practice—both the situated interpretive demands placed on the respondents and the resources and orientations that were relevant and available. The respondents' past experience was, of course, crucial to their present formulations, but how it was narratively assembled was a local matter.

From the researcher's standpoint, these interviews represent concerted efforts to collect actively assembled interpretations of experience that address particular research agendas. In the first interview situation, for example, the respondent was asked if she would articulate significant events of her past into some sort of continuous course, convoluted as it might be. The interviewer suggested general ways of orienting to the narrative task at hand, inviting narrative associations between mundane and momentous occasions to capture a more or less continuous, if tangled, flow of life. In the second interview project, the vocabulary of *milestones*, *turning points*, and *crises* provoked narratives consisting of momentous events, necessarily demanding that they be portrayed as something other than mundane.

The two interviews are not comparable in the sense that they fail to provide standardized, neutral catalysts for the respondents' stories. But the crucial analytic point is that the interviewers guided and constrained the conversation so as to produce narratives that were appropriate to their projects *without* dictating how the respondents' lives might be portrayed within the operative interpretive framework and language. There is always an operative interpretive framework, not the least of which is the "neutral" frame touted in standardized interviewing. Although the respective interviewers certainly contributed to alternative forms of storytelling, the stories told were no less authentic, no less reflective of subjects' "actual" experience than they would have been if the respondents had been incited by ostensibly more neutral questions and probes. We might think of the interviewers' participation as keeping the respondents' speech "on narrative course," asking the respondents to interrogate their own experiences in particular ways and pointing respondents in fruitful interpretive directions.

As life stories, the key to analyzing these data is to treat them as a form of *biographical work* conducted jointly by interviewer and respondent within the context of the interview (Gubrium & Holstein, 1995; Gubrium et al., 1994). The interviewer, in a sense, challenges the respondent to produce a coherent life narrative out of a designated, limited stock of mutually relevant resources. The result is the respondent's artful but culturally grounded construction, assembled, in practice, out of the interpretive materials and orientations at hand. Like all interview data, life stories do not simply await discovery and articulation, but are constituted within the interactional context of the interview, drawing on both situationally relevant and long-standing resources.

6. CONSTRUCTING MEANING WITHIN THE INTERVIEW

As we noted, the research topic establishes parameters of interest from the start of an interview, broadly framing the subject matter of forthcoming questions. Both the interviewer and the respondent assume that the respondent's answers and comments will orient to varied aspects of the topic, not unrelated matters. The meaning of what emerges is then actively constructed within the interview interaction. The interpretation of questions and the meaningful content of responses is not settled once and for all at the start or as various topics and their related questions are introduced. Meaning-making is a continually unfolding process.

Interview Format and Meaning-Making Visibility

Important aspects of meaning-making remain invisible in interviews with highly structured formats. When respondents are given fixed alternatives from which to choose, it is difficult to know to what in their stocks of knowledge the alternatives will be linked. Take, for example, two respondents who answer a fixed-choice question about satisfaction with family income. Response options range from being very satisfied to very dissatisfied. Say that both respondents answer that they are very satisfied with their family incomes. Does this suggest that they carry the same sentiments about the matter, that their responses have the same experiential meaning? The fixed format does not tell us whether, for example, the first respondent links her satisfaction with an objectively low family income that she nonetheless figures to be greater than the family income of her older sister who is a long-standing family rival in financial affairs. The second respondent may link her "identical" satisfaction with a desire to stay at home raising her children, not wanting to enter the labor force in order to increase the family's income. The respondents' respective *narrative linkages*, which are rendered invisible by the interview format, make ostensibly identical responses into disparate parts of distinct life stories.

In general, the more standardized the interview, the less visible are such meaning-making linkages. The standard Likert-type response format is exemplary in this regard. The response options include only the following: strongly agree, agree, neutral, disagree, and strongly disagree. Presumably, the format presents a full range of generalized options for responding to an interview item. Still, although the respondent may, for instance, strongly disagree, the format offers no way to know the subjective sense of the respondent's strong disagreement. To tap subjectively meaningful differences, survey researchers can, and do, offer questions with a choice of answers generated from pretests or other preliminary studies. For example, preliminary studies might have found that when respondents are asked their views of parenting, responses tend to fall into three or four categories. One category might consist of responses referring to the respondents' parents' kind of parenting, such as the desire to duplicate or resist how one's own parents dealt with their children. Such preliminary responses can eventually warrant establishing a general response category for those who say that they take their own parents into account in thinking about parenting.

But, although substantive response options may be empirically generated, they still suppress the linkages that respondents make in the course of being interviewed. Selecting the response option of taking one's own parents into account, whether as positive or negative models, does not reveal the complexities involved in communicating such sentiments. For example, the respondent who is asked in a more open interview format to explain why she always thinks about what her parents did when disciplining their own children might give an answer similar to one a mother conveyed during a discussion of parenting during a parent effectiveness class:

> It depends. When my kids are really bad, I mean really bad, that's when I think how my mother used to do with us. You know, don't spare the rod or something like that in those days? But, usually, I feel that Mother was too harsh with us and I think that that kind of punishment isn't good for kids today. Better to talk about it and iron things out that way. Still, like I say, it depends on how you want to think about it, doesn't it?

The "it depends" feature of the response suggests that standardization obscures the narratively contextual character of meaning-making. To convey a narrative is to tell a story about the subject matter and selves under consideration, embedding what is being talked about in further talk (see Taylor, 1989; Riessman, 1993). The speaker conveys how experiences relate to each other, elaborating on how the relationship came about, when it did, and why. In this regard, we might interpret this mother's statement as, initially, the beginning of a story about her thoughts and feelings concerning parenting "when [her] children are really bad." In this story, the mother comments that she thinks about parenting, especially discipline, in terms of what her own mother did. Her response is given meaning within an emergent chronicle of contingent intergenerational emulation. If she had continued with the story— to develop its plot—she might have made narrative linkages with, say, the rampant breakdown of discipline in today's generation, something that, she could have added, was "just not there" in her parent's era. The mother paraphrased the maxim "spare the rod and spoil the child" in support of such sentiments. In other words, the story she began to tell, whose sentiments could easily coincide with an empirically generated interview response option, had a beginning, was developing into a middle, and could have led to a quite rationally elaborated end.

But the mother then shifted narrative gears, as it were. Her initial, inchoate story brought to the foreground the misbehavior of children in relation to generational differences. In that narrative context, her own mother served as a positive model for parenting, providing a stock of knowledge for a story about how present-day parents might handle unruly children. Shortly thereafter, the phrase "but, usually" (following the introductory "it depends") initiated a contextual shift in which punishment rather than misbehavior was narratively foregrounded. In that narrative context, the mother's evaluation of her own mother's discipline produced a negative model, of someone prone to exacting excess punishment. The story now centered on punishment, not misbehavior, the developing plot of which communicated preferred alternatives for misbehaving children. Punishment was tacitly divided into two categories—corporal and rational—and the mother stated that, currently, rational retribution was more effective; the kind of punishment her mother exacted would not be "good for kids today."

At the end of the extract, we have the makings of yet another narrative shift. The mother repeated "it depends," explaining what it depended on, which amounted to "how you want to think about it." This not only signaled the equally compelling narrative force of two quite different stories, with distinctive implications for self plot development, and contrasting consequences for disciplinary action, but it also evinced narrative reflexivity. The mother virtually told her listeners that she was not just a narrator led on by the stories to be told; she also conveyed that she was *aware* that she was actively involved in deciding which story to tell.

This latter comment constituted a kind of story about stories. Broadly, the comment was about the agency or activeness of the storyteller and, particularly, the consideration that storytellers need to decide which story to tell among the stories to be told about children's misbehavior and parental discipline. Brief as it was, this latter part was an inchoate story in its own right, implicating an important storytelling decision. It showed that the mother, as the active interview respondent she was, not only told stories as responses but constructed the relevance of possible responses at the same time.

Needless to say, a fixed-choice interview format would render such narrative complexity invisible. But so would a precoded, open-ended format. A respondent who, like the mother above, speaks at length of parenting, would be coded according to the appropriate precoded category. What is impossible to precode is the narrative shifting evident in the mother's statement, where the same person takes different positions in formulating answers to the questions and subject matter at hand. If precodes were indeed used to classify such a response, the mother in this instance would have had to be coded as *both* "parent-oriented" and "not parent-oriented," which, of course, fixed codes of any kind, let alone precodes, cannot accommodate. In practice, her response would be rendered useless, eliminated as technically meaningless. To make matters worse, the open-endedness of the interview notwithstanding, precoding would automatically preclude the mother's insight about how she constructs and manages the choices (stories) before her, in this instance rendering the mother's narrative reflexivity invisible.

Narrative complexity requires an interview format that accommodates contextual shifts and reflexivity. Rather than suppressing the respondent's and the interviewer's reflexivity, the active interviewer encourages contextual shifts and reflections. The respondent is not treated as a judgmental dope, as Garfinkel (1967) put it, but is heard to speak of life in relation to diverse substantive and perspectival contingencies. Respondents' reflexive comments are endogenous guides to their narrative identities.

The active interview takes seriously what respondents sometimes virtually tell their listeners, namely, that life is as much storied as it is lived (see Ochberg, 1994; Sarbin, 1986). Respondents convey this when they state that they have to think things over from their various perspectives, that there are diverse contexts for interpretation in life, or that they need to take certain matters into account in deciding how they feel

56

and what to say. Facilitating the narrative construction of responses, the active interviewer orients to respondents' lives as storied and managed by, and through, narrative.

In practice, this means that interview schedules should be guides at best, not scripts, for the give-and-take of the interview process. Schedules need sufficient flexibility to be substantively built up and altered in the course of the interview. New questions and discussion items are added or combined as the interview unfolds, according to the organization and diversity of meanings being conveyed. The respondent might even be asked what kinds of questions he or she thinks should be posed. The interviewer would encourage the respondent to explain why such questions made sense, simultaneously attending to the narrative contingencies and reflexivity of explanations.

Lest we forget that interviews center on specific research topics, the active interview should not be seen as just another conversation; not just anything goes. Focused on interpretive practice, the active interview study has two key aims: to gather information about *what* the research project is about and to explicate *how* knowledge concerning that topic is narratively constructed. Findings, then, come in two intertwined forms: data about the subject matter of the research and data about how that subject matter is organized in respondents' narrative experiences.

Indigenous Coding

In practice, both interviewer and respondent continuously engage in coding experience. In contrast to the coding done in standard survey research, active coding is indigenous to the interview; it takes places and unfolds as an integral part of the interview process, not just beforehand or afterward. When an interviewer asks a respondent, for example, about preferred parenting styles, the interviewer already codes domestic reality in a particular way by linking the behavior of parents with diverse patterns of conduct toward children, asking the respondent to select his or her style among available options. Assuming a stock of knowledge that includes multiple conceptions of parenting makes it reasonable to pose such a question and, of course, takes for granted that the respondent shares the stock and can meaningfully designate a style.

But consider the woman who, after the above question was posed, asked:

I don't know what you mean by the ways you can parent. You mean what I do when my kids act up? You just do what you have to, what anyone would, I guess. I don't know. You know, get 'em to behave. Put a stop to it. If they're fighting, take over and make sure no one gets hurt. You don't have much choice, do you? Do what any parent would do. That kind of thing?

The respondent was admittedly confused and tried herself to meaningfully code "the ways" of parenting. She described concretely what she did when children "act up"—what she claimed any good parent would do—and offered an example of how one responds.

Immediately following this, the interviewer sought clarification by answering that she wondered what style of parenting or strategy the respondent used, for instance, in dealing with difficult children. In the subsequent exchange, it became evident in the interviewer's and respondent's questions, answers, and mutual clarifications that the interviewer was employing a different stock of knowledge than the respondent. The interviewer aimed for an answer derived from the perspective of a respondent who oriented to parenting options. The interviewer was not trying to put words in the respondent's mouth or ideas in her head, as it were; she was merely tacitly conveying that the stock of knowledge from which this and related questions were formulated was built around a code of options.

The respondent, on the other hand, answered concretely from what she took for granted to be "any parent's" point of view and, accordingly, described what she or any parent would do. She spoke substantively about parenting, in terms of what she did when her children misbehaved, not in relation to alternative courses of action or strategies. Her stock of knowledge at the moment did not appear to code parenting in terms of options. As the respondent answered, she was simultaneously searching for narrative footing. Phrases such as "you mean?" and "that kind of thing?" signaled that the respondent was trying to get a handle on an unfamiliar or problematic experiential code. As interviewer and respondent sought common narrative ground, contextual issues repeatedly complicated matters.

Active interviewing orients to, systematically notices, and gathers data on the simultaneous coding and construction of knowledge within the interview. The active interviewer manages the interview to take account of differential coding schemes, gathering as much data about contrasting narrative contexts and linkages as about substantive matters. In the preceding interview, the active interviewer would come away from the interview with data not only about what the respondent said in response to an interview item about parenting but also about how what was said was meaningfully constructed by the respondent in relation to the interviewer's questions. Such data on interpretive practice reveal the diverse narrative linkages that constitute interview meanings. They can show, for example, how a respondent might interpret the "same" substantive data quite differently from another respondent, or how the "same" respondent, taking alternate narrative positions, might incorporate those data into quite different stories relating to parenting styles.

Horizons of Meaning

Coherent, meaningful configurations emerge through patterned narrative linkages. We refer to these patterns as *horizons of meaning*. For example, the parent effectiveness class participant we quoted earlier on the subject of disciplining children offered incipient linkages that, if they coherently developed into full-blown stories, would have given rise to two separate horizons of meaning for the related sentiments and actions conveyed regarding the matter under consideration. These horizons provide narrative contexts that suggest other linkages. Horizons and linkages are mutually constitutive, reflexively relating patterns to their constituent parts and connections. The "same" elements of experience can be arranged into differing configurations, taking on contrasting meanings as they coalesce in relation to distinct horizons.

A primary objective of active interviewing is to promote the visibility of linkages and horizons. As we have argued, standardized interviewing techniques often make ungrounded assumptions about how respondents orient to interview topics and questions. Proceeding on those assumptions amounts to a willingness to ignore the active process by which respondents make linkages, assemble horizons, and generally orient to the interpretive tasks at hand. Standardized survey research imposes horizons of meaning from the start by way of precedent-setting introductions, transitions, and questions (see Chapter 5), being content to gloss over alternative linkages that respondents might develop themselves. Without examining the linkages that constitute answers to survey questions, researchers remain in the dark as to just what meanings were assigned to the questions posed, how those assignments were made, and what narrative resources were mobilized to execute the process.

Active interviewing capitalizes on the ways that respondents both develop and use horizons to establish and organize subjective meanings. In actively encouraging respondents' narratives, the interviewer invites the respondent to fashion stories that, in their content and connections, reveal how the respondent structures experiential meaning. By manipulating emergent horizons—suggesting subjective relevancies, orientations, and connections—the interviewer interpretively challenges the respondent to make sense of experience in relation to various subjective possibilities. Offering up diverse horizons and possibilities for narrative linkage are active techniques for making visible those meaning-making processes that standard interviewing ignores or obscures.

Collaborative Construction

Interviewer and respondent collaboratively construct the meaning of interview narratives. To illustrate, let us consider in detail the linkages and horizons of meaning in an interview taken from a study of the subjective quality of older persons' lives (Gubrium, 1993). The research was conducted in various residential settings, including nursing homes, adult congregate living facilities, and mixed-age neighborhoods. All interviews began with a request to the respondent to briefly tell his or her life story. The goal was to get respondents in each setting to think about life as an experiential object that one might examine and evaluate in its varied dimensions. It was important to actively and systematically target how respondents constructed what they communicated both in the life story and throughout the interview in relation to their present circumstances. Although a set of general questions guided the interview, the format accommodated, even encouraged, shifts in context and alternate narrative linkages. The interviewer, at times, even provoked such shifts as a means of making visible the ways the respondent could subjectively code and convey the quality of a life.

The following extracts are taken from an interview completed by one of the authors (JG) with Helen Cody (HC), who lived at Frampton Place, an adult congregate-living facility consisting of several houses and small blocks of apartment buildings located in a parklike setting. Helen was 88 years old and had lived in her apartment at Frampton for 3 years.

Despite being a bit forgetful, she managed on her own quite well. Helen's interview, which lasted over an hour, can be divided into four parts in terms of the narrative horizons informing her discussion of the quality of life. The first part, the flavor of which is conveyed in the next three extracts, is the recurrent narrative of a fond past. The quality of her life in this part of the interview was jointly constructed against a horizon of happy memories of figure skating, contrasted with a lonely present. The interview began this way:

JG: Everyone has a life story. I wonder if you can tell me a bit about your life?

HC: Well, I was born in Providence, Rhode Island, and my uncle was the first figure skater in the country and he taught me figure skating. And I skated in the Boston area five opening nights and so there's that era. And then, of course, I just was married and had my son and not much else. I don't know what else to talk about. And then I, then after my husband died, I came on here to be near my son. So that's about it.

JG: If you could divide your life up into chapters, let's say you were writing your life story and you had chapters, what would the different chapters be about? What would, for example, Chapter 1 be about?

HC: Well, my youth was very interesting. I did figure skating and dancing and things like that. That was a happy time, with my uncle.

JG: And what would another chapter be about?

HC: I can't tell. Not much of anything. Just my life, just my life. I can't think of anything else. I haven't done too much, just living and doing my health work and what have you and having friends come in and things like that. That's about all. I've lived a quiet life outside of my youth when I was skating and was in the limelight.

At the interviewer's suggestion, Helen elaborated on her skating experience. When the interviewer returned to the book-and-chapter metaphor, using that as a framework to get Helen to think comparatively and in the long term, Helen elaborated on the contrast between her current loneliness, the "old crabs" around her, and her "more interesting" life and younger personal attitude.

JG: What would the last chapter of your life [story] be about, if you were writing it?

HC: Well, I don't know. Just that I'm here.

JG: Where?

HC: Right here in [pause] . . .

JG: In Frampton, you mean?

HC: No, not Frampton. [Pause] Well, of course. I'm not too happy with all the old folks. They're really old and I'm not in that class at all. I stand out because, well, I have my senses you know, and everything. I'm more interested in everything and so it isn't very interesting to me, the old folks. And they're old crabs, most of them. And the women. If they don't like you or think you're just wrong, they shun you and everything. Women are something really, they are. Especially with their own. And they're crabby and probably always very crabby. . . . So I sort of lived alone here. There's one or two people I can converse with, but they don't, you know, they're too old or something, you know. And they don't take that interest in visiting.

JG: That's important to you?

HC: Yes, it's important to me. So I have to sort of live alone, whether I like it or not. [Elaborates.] I think if you have had an interesting life, you'd be more talkative when you're older, or interesting, but they never had that. So, of course, I kind of expect it. They just go their one way, so it isn't very happy here for me because I don't feel old, you see. So that's what's hard. I never would be old. I'm old now, but I never feel it, you know, so that's tough.

As the interview unfolded, there were other distinguishable and contrasting narrative linkages with Helen's interesting past. Probing for particulars that conveyed the current quality of Helen's life, the interviewer asked if there was anyone at Frampton whom Helen thought of as family. She responded with an emphatic no, linking that with Frampton residents' lack of intelligence and their not having had the "full life" she had. The question of age was broached and Helen repeated that she did not feel old. She was sorely disappointed that so many around her acted and seemed to think like old people. She spoke of craving for contact and conversation with others. She repeatedly recalled her youth, and, at one point, there was an extended discussion of her now-deceased husband and her only child, a son, who was 60 years old and lived nearby with his wife.

Asked the meaning of the word *home*, Helen returned to linkages that formed the developing the narrative horizon of her story:

Well, home means everything I think, because it is home. If you make it a home, but you have to make it a home. And enjoy it. I'd like a lot of people coming in and visiting. Being normal, you know, instead of the woman next door who doesn't even speak to me. I don't even know her. See how ignorant it is here? When I came here, I saw there was a woman next door and I went over to see her and I said, "I thought I'd say hello to you." And she says, "I don't want anything to do with you." She didn't even know me! And she talks against me and everything and she doesn't even know me. Ignorant!

But as she discussed home, a new horizon of meaning emerged, marking a shift in the context from which Helen spoke of her life. It became apparent that in the context of Frampton Place and its residents, Helen did not feel at home and the quality of her life was decidedly negative; the linkages between Frampton Place, its occupants, and the quality of her life formed one horizon. But, when the discussion shifted contexts to what Helen, like others, called her "things"—referring to long-standing and meaningful possessions, particularly her furniture—Helen felt quite positively "at home" at Frampton Place, as the following exchange shows.

JG: Now that you've lived here for about 3 years, I think, do you feel it's home now?

HC: No, because of the people. This is my home [points to her things], just this house here.

JG: But you feel this [points to surroundings] is home?

HC: Yes, it has to be 'cause some of my furniture is here, but my son took the rest of my stuff to put in storage. So this just [pause] . . . there's two bedrooms here.

JG: Are there? [Helen shows the interviewer around.] Oh, yeah, I see. What would it have to be like to be more like home here? You [said] you feel like home here in this place?

HC: Well, just because it's my furniture.

As the interviewer actively probed the linkages between place, possessions, and home, the quality of Helen's life, as she portrayed it earlier in the interview, began to change dramatically. Until now, the horizon of meaning for the quality of her life was constructed from linkages with Frampton Place, overaged residents, and isolation, which, in turn, were repeatedly contrasted with Helen's earlier life. The newly emerging linkages of home provided the interviewer the opportunity to explore

an alternative narrative horizon, namely, the home immediately surrounding Helen. As it turned out, if this had been the exclusive focus
of an interview with Helen about the quality of her life, the interview
would have revealed that quality more positively.

Note how, in the following extracts from what became a distinctly
separate part of the interview in terms of its particular linkages, a new
narrative horizon incited Helen to speak rather glowingly about her life.
The interviewer further prompted Helen by using an item from the
interview guide asking whether one's present living situation is considered part of one's life, which affirmed a link between the quality of life
and Helen's immediate surroundings.

JG: Do you feel this place [pointing to the surroundings], living here, is part
of your life or is it separate from your life?

HC: No, it's part of my life, on account of the furniture. It feels like home,
because it's my furniture, because if I don't have my furniture, I don't
feel very much at home.

JG: Is that right?

HC: Yeah, I think if you had it all your life, you would. And had to give it up,
you wouldn't. [Points to various objects in the room.] My little details and
everything. [Picks up a picture she painted.] So anyway [pointing out
varied details of the picture], that is in Bromfield, Connecticut. That's the
first law school in the country.

JG: In that picture there?

HC: Yeah.

JG: You painted that, didn't you?

HC: Yes, I painted all of these. [Respondent and interviewer scan various
objects in the room.] And my husband was a lawyer and so I've been in
that first law school in the country and I painted it. My son painted that
bird. He has the artistic streak. You get the perspective. See how he's got
the house down below. He has, [pause] his judgment is good with the
painting. The house is below, the bird's up in the tree, for perspective.

As Helen described the paintings and other objects in the room, her
experience came alive in a story of a person who took great satisfaction
from life. Asked what meaning the things had for her, Helen answered,
"Oh, everything, everything. They're my life, my folks. They were good
people, very good." The quality of that life was now narratively con-
nected with her things, as she called them, forming a horizon for further,

detailed linkages by both Helen and the interviewer. Asked how the paintings and other objects figured in her life, Helen explained:

> Well, I wonder how they ever did [related activities]. Now I'm enjoying them. I sit here and look at boats [in the pictures] and everything. I've taken a lot of enjoyment in them. I've given a lot away and, you know, that's that.

A brief exchange immediately following this comment produced another shift in context. Turning away from the pictures, other objects, and her immediate surroundings, Helen returned to speak of the quality of her life in the terms used in the first part of the interview. The transition occurred this way, prompted by a question about what it would mean not to have her things surrounding her.

JG: Are these [things] very important to have around you, these things?

HC: Oh, yes, well because they were something I did, you know. No, I think it was wonderful that I could do it, you know. It's been good that I could do something that I could enjoy. So I've enjoyed those things.

JG: What would it be like if you lived here without all these things?

HC: Well, I wouldn't have those memories. They've been good memories, of my life, happy times. So, anyway, it's no fun to get old because you are lonesome, especially when people aren't friendly. That's doubly hard. That's the hardest thing I think I can put up with. People's actions, they speak louder than words. The old saying: actions speak louder than words.

Narrative linkages again cast the give-and-take of the interview in terms of loneliness, the "old crabs" in Helen's midst, and the contrasting, pleasant remembrances of things past. Each interview topic now drew negative evaluations, formed against the reinstituted horizon of meaning.

Finally, a further shift in context led to a fourth part of the interview. Centered on one or two Frampton friends who played bingo together, life now was a story filled with laughter. Like the other transitions, this one was accomplished in collaboration with the interviewer. Note how, in the following extract, the interviewer helped to shift the narrative to "people that you enjoy," prompting its particular linkages and horizons of meaning. The extract followed a question about the kinds of problems Helen would imagine there might be if she lived in a nursing home.

JG: What kinds of problems do you have in mind?

HC: People being mean, especially women. I wouldn't want to be with a bunch of women. They're very nasty and jealous. If you look too good or something, yeah, they're very nasty. I haven't seen many. . . . There is one or two around here I've seen that are very, very nice, though, and laughs and enjoys herself. But [here] there isn't many like her. No.

JG: So there are some people that you enjoy?

HC: Oh, yes, yes. I go down there to eat occasionally [in the congregate dining room]. I don't care for their food, so that's why I cook my own.

JG: Do you have any meals down there at all?

HC: No, I don't. Once in a while, I go down if they play bingo or something like that. That's fun. People laugh there when we do those things, a game or something. I go to games. I like those 'cause people usually laugh. Some never laugh at anything. So, anyway, I go there and there's this one lovely old woman. She is lovable. She is really lovely, laughs, is pleasant, you know. She's a joy to know. Most of them are sourpusses. [Elaborates.]

The multiple shifts in this interview illustrate active collaboration between interviewer and respondent. Their give-and-take indicated that much more went on than a simple vessel-of-answers view would suggest. Narrative shifts produced different contexts within which questions were asked and answered, producing categorically diverse meanings.

7. MULTIVOCALITY AND MULTIPLE RESPONDENTS

What if we take seriously the notion that the interview comprises multiple exchanges between and among varied positions or points of view? In the preceding interview with Helen Cody, we might say that, narratively, more than one respondent and one interviewer participated, making the interview a *multivocal* occasion. Why not also extend this to other actual voices that might contribute to the meaning-making process? This would mean including in the same interview, say, the caregiver who prefers to speak as a daughter and another caregiver who currently articulates caregiving in the voice of a mother, resulting in two different respondents. This also applies to interviewers. For example, we can imagine the participation of two interviewers, one attending mainly to the *whats* and the other to the *hows* of the interview. This introduces a new element of communicative leadership, providing a way of encouraging and monitoring different lines of narrative production. It is not that such differences cannot be examined as a dialogical feature of individual interviews, but the narrative force of multivocality may be more poignant and visible when it is a matter of the individual commitments of several participants, where particular identities consistently organize responses.

Consider what is discovered in respondents' stocks of knowledge when the interview's multivocality includes actual co-respondents. The following two examples are drawn from interviews conducted as part of ethnographic studies, but the general idea may be extended to survey designs, in which diverse and varied combinations of respondents are included. The kind of narrative contribution that actual others make in interviews, of course, is an empirical matter. Although the following examples show how productive the inclusion of others can be in making visible the complex, relational character of the experiences under consideration, including others can also suppress multivocality. The general point is that the active interview permits such concerns and research options to be considered and adopted; it does not restrict them as a matter of methodological convenience or principle.

Including a Spouse

Our first example shows how the inclusion of a spouse in the interview can shape the narrative linkages used to convey a life story and describe the quality of life in a nursing facility. As part of the quality-of-life research discussed earlier (Gubrium, 1993), interviews were conducted with widowed, single, and still-married residents living together. A theme of the research was that the quality of life of the nursing home takes on its meaning in relation to lifelong experiences. For example, the quality of nursing home life for a resident who had "never had a home to speak of" might contrast considerably with that of the resident of the same facility who looked back on the "sweetest home this side of heaven."

The example is drawn from an engaging interview with a married couple, Don and Sue Hughes, who shared a room at the Westside Care Center, a nursing home. Sue was 81 and Don 88 years old. Don was the formally designated respondent, but the life story requested of him at the start, which would eventually be used to explore narrative linkages with the quality of the couple's nursing home life, was constructed with Sue's help. As the interview unfolded, it soon was apparent that Sue did not much like Don's version of things because it did not include her; Don told his story as if Sue were missing from his life. Chiming in, Sue quickly reconstructed the narrative horizon that they eventually used to form the evaluative linkages of their current circumstances.

The interviewer (I) began by asking Don to describe his life:

I: [To Don] I was hoping you'd tell me about your life.
Don: I was a hobo!
I: You were a hobo.
Sue: [To Don] Why don't you tell her where you were born?
Don: I was born in Minnesota and I left when I was 16 years old.
Sue: Go on. So why did you leave?
Don: Just to bum, see the country. So we went, another boy and myself. We went out west on the Northern Pacific Railroad. We was supposed to help put in signal posts. We worked there for a while and then went to Sheridan, Wyoming, and went from there up to the mountains. After that, we came home riding the rails. I stayed home for a couple of years and then a buddy

of mine says, "Let's go to Florida." At that time, I says, "No." I knew a girl and her father was moving to California and he asked me if I'd drive his Ford there and I said, "Sure." So a buddy and me drove out to California, but when we got to the desert, the car broke down. We fixed it and drove to Sacramento. [Elaborates on his life in California and, later, his life "going East," and finally going to Florida.] We finally got down to Florida. He [Don's buddy] had been in the army and the government was allocating homestead exemptions in Florida at the time. He thought he might want one. We looked all over and there was nothing but swampland where we looked. So I came to this part of Florida here and we both were working. That's where I met my wife and that's the end of my life story.

Sue: [Sarcastically] Why don't you tell her that we got married in the meantime? I'm part of it, too, you know.

As Don continued, Sue teasingly insisted that the story tell of their life together. Although his initial version dwelled on work experiences and "bummin' around," at Sue's insistence the story began to include marriage and family living. We return to the interview as Don concluded a lengthy description of his many years working as a masonry contractor.

I: Was this after the Depression?

Don: The Depression was [pause] . . .

Sue: It was just over.

Don: I walked 10 miles to work for 10 cents an hour. But you know I had a family and I wasn't lazy. But, anyway, after I worked for this fella, we had a big snowstorm. [Elaborates.] So we decided to come back to Florida. [Elaborates.] We enjoyed life. She [Sue] had penicillin poisoning a couple of times. When I retired, I thought we had money to last.

Sue: You forgot to tell her one thing, that we built our own home stick by stick and every nail.

Don: Yeah. Anyway, our money didn't last. I got so's I couldn't work too much anymore and she got sick two or three more times.

Sue: [Chuckling] Just listen to him. In the meantime we had three more children. [Sarcastically] Remember that?

Don: Yeah, in the meantime we had three more children. That's all. That's it.

Sue: [Laughing] That's it? You're joking.

Following this, Don and Sue openly collaborated in describing their lives. It became clear that, in Sue's words, they "did all the things together." The story now became *theirs*, not just a narrative of Don's individual experiences, as the following extract illustrates.

Don: [Chuckling.] This much I can tell ya. We've been married 63 years and enjoyed every bit of it. We worked together and never left. For instance, she had a bunch of girlfriends and she never went out at night. And I had boyfriends and I wouldn't go out at night. If we went to any place, we went together.

Sue: We traveled together. We went all over the country together. We didn't have such a bad life. We loved to camp. We loved to fish. We loved to do all kinds of outdoor sports. We like baseball, football. Name it. And we did all the things together. We never went to one place and let the other fella go another place.

The interview next turned to the nursing home. Although the couple's life together before placement had its disappointments, Don and Sue resented certain aspects of nursing home living even more, qualities they claimed to be worse than any earlier hardship. Yet it was evident, too, that one thing sustained the good life for them, something that Sue had made sure was conveyed as part of their life story: togetherness.

Although Don and Sue teased each other and conjured up their respective foibles, they repeatedly affirmed their mutual affectionate bond. The nursing home's shortcomings became marginal to the "sassiness" they called out in each other. As the following extract shows, Sue and Don were more than nursing home residents judgmentally attuned to their surroundings; they were, and would continue to be, the sassy couple they had delighted in being over the years. The long-standing linkages of togetherness, which Sue's collaboration with Don in the interview revealed, cast the nursing home's quality of life in a way the stock of knowledge presented in Don's story might never have shown. If Don's initial story had provided the horizon of meaning for the interview's narrative linkages, what Don mentions in the following extract as the nursing home's prisonlike quality of life would have contrasted mightily with his youthful free-spiritedness, casting the facility quite negatively. The narrative influence of Sue's intrusions, however, lessened the contrast, conveying the present quality of their lives as more sassily benign.

Don: [Chuckling.] I was a no-good bum.

Sue: He's no bum. We're just as close as we were before and I love him. He's the only thing that makes this place tolerable. But he gets sassy sometimes and I have to knock him down a peg or two, but other than that, we still have fun together. He plays cribbage and cheats, but we still manage to get by. We gab and blab, about the old days, you know. That keeps us goin'.

Don: But this isn't the place for us. That's all I can say. It's too much like prison. If I didn't have her, I'd go crazy and so would she. [Elaborates.] At least we have each other.

Sue: I know, dear. We've had a good life, but now we're bitching like the devil. [Chuckling.] I hope that isn't on the tape.

I: Well, it is.

Don: [To Sue, sarcastically.] You mean to say you're not "itching" now?

Sue: [Chuckling.] I didn't say "itching." I said "bitching." We still manage to giggle.

Group Interviews

If the narrative force of significant others helps shape the stock of knowledge accessed by interview participants, consider the parallel force of group interviews. One variation, the focus group, is usually composed of 5 to 10 participants, who, with the guidance of a moderator, discuss a topic such as the advantages and disadvantages of particular marketing strategies. In academic research, the moderator is often the researcher him- or herself. Self-help movements often encourage or sponsor a second type of group interview—the support group. Although organized much like focus groups, support group discussions tend to center more on personal troubles that participants may be experiencing. Support groups are primarily organized to help participants, but they can also serve as a highly active interview format (see Gubrium, 1986).

Morgan (1988) lists the visibility of interaction as one of main advantages of group interviews. The parries and challenges of group discussion highlight the agreements and disagreements in a particular population. As Morgan points out, the give-and-take of group interviews allow diverse categorizations and sentiments to emerge, showing how participants flesh out, alter, or reconstruct viewpoints in response to challenges. Group interviews also display in bold relief the local inventiveness of the interview process, displaying emerging and complex narrative linkages and the diversity of narrative horizons.

In this regard, consider the multivocality of support groups for the family caregivers of Alzheimer's disease sufferers, studied as part of research on the descriptive organization of senility (Gubrium, 1986). Some of the groups were comprised of caregiving spouses, mainly the elderly wives of people with dementia cared for at home. A few groups were limited to the adult children of parents with dementia, usually caregiving daughters. Most groups included a mixture of family caregivers, significant others, and the rare sibling or friend who provided care.

As group participants told their separate stories and conveyed particular caregiving experiences, it was evident that the interactions contributed to the development of shared stocks of knowledge. These "local cultures" were formed by group participants and conveyed common meaning in the context of group discussion (Gubrium, 1989). Just as organizational researchers have taken account of personal narrative, shared stories, and collective symbols to shed light on organizational decision making (Jones, Moore, & Snyder, 1988), the local cultures of the support groups provided narrative resources for the meanings and choices participants linked with caregiving. Each participant was a potential respondent in relation to others and to local culture, making group discussions tantamount to shared interviewing. This was apparent in the various questions, answers, interpretations, and positional shifts. In many ways, the proceedings more naturally resembled the complex multivocality of everyday life than the standard, individual interview.

In one support group, the notion of the "really" ideal caregiver was a persistent narrative resource, presenting a local basis for evaluating individual caregiving responsibilities. A legendary caregiver, Jessica, who no longer attended but was influential in community Alzheimer's disease service activities, was a virtual exemplar of "total devotion." Jessica presented participants with a standard by which they might compare and convey their own caregiving activity, felt strain, and sentiments about possible nursing home placement. Participants used Jessica's experience to assess whether their individual contributions were "all that great" compared to "what Jessica does for her husband."

In use, the image of Jessica's caregiving was not always positive. When group members considered the condition known as "denial," which is a tacit refusal to acknowledge the reality of an event or experience, Jessica became an exemplar of overdevotion. This brought to bear a contrasting horizon of meaning for speaking of familial responsibility. Against the horizon of denial, Jessica was still referenced as an ideal, but one *not* to be emulated. In this context, Jessica was used to evaluate whether, in comparison, one was being realistic about continued home care. The question became whether one had gone "too far," that is, to a point where a totally devoted caregiver becomes the disease's so-called second victim, caught in a spiral of overconcern and the denial of personal and domestic strain.

Jessica's exemplary status in the group offered support for diametrically opposed sentiments regarding nursing home placement. When Jessica represented the positive ideal, participants hesitated to speak of the possibility of placing their demented loved ones in a nursing home. The narrative force of this horizon led participants to speak of those who were too (coldly) rational in assessing their home situation as rushing to judgment—deciding selfishly that it was time to consider an alternative to home care. When Jessica was cast as the negative ideal, participants discussed the indirect and insidious impact of dementia on the caregiver and other members of the household. In this context, one was likely to hear participants entertain denial as underpinning overdevotion.

Depending on the issue under consideration, either devotion or denial, Jessica's legendary status narratively shifted—virtually "escaping" (Silverman, 1989)—from being a positive, to being a negative, standard of comparison. Paralleling this, participants who used Jessica as a basis for evaluating their own caregiving experienced rather dramatic alterations in understanding themselves, their circumstances, and others' thoughts and feelings.

Actual multivocality broadens interview data immeasurably. In our first example, Sue entered the interview as a significant other, shaping and extending the narrative horizons available for speaking of the quality of care well beyond what Don was constructing on his own. In our second example, the narrative force of local culture served, through its speakers, to differentiate the linkages and meanings of caregiving responsibility in complex ways. Although the ongoing positioning and reflexivity of individual interviews convey varying horizons of meaning in their own right, actual multivocality can emphasize the richness of meaning revealed in the active interview.

8. RETHINKING INTERVIEW PROCEDURES

As we noted at the start, our perspective offers a distinctive way of construing the interview. The active approach is more than an inventory of methods; it is a theoretical stance toward data collection and analysis. Still, research procedures are implicated. In this concluding chapter, we outline how select procedures are rethought in relation to the active interview.

Topic Selection

What one decides to study has methodological consequences. The simple way to approach this is to say that some topics lend themselves more readily to particular techniques, whereas alternate procedures may be more appropriate for other topics. Although certainly true, this suggests that one's method of inquiry is separate and distinct from empirical phenomena. As we have argued and illustrated, however, the phenomenon can virtually emerge in the course of inquiry, in response to the research itself. In this regard, one's methodological approach unavoidably shapes what the phenomenon can potentially be, and vice versa. Put slightly differently, the way that one construes the topic under consideration both dictates and is shaped by one's strategies for empirical observation. Active interviewing, then, can develop its topics as much from indigenous activities and meanings as from preexisting interests or preestablished agendas (see DeVault, 1990, for specifically feminist implications).

Standard interviewing is perhaps most appropriate for generating straightforward behavioral or demographic information, especially when the categories of inquiry are well defined and familiar (e.g., respondents' age, sex, or place of birth). But, as we have seen, even the most standardized, seemingly uninvolved interviews can be deceptively active. Active interviewing brings meaning and its construction to the foreground. An active approach might therefore be most appropriate in those instances when the researcher is interested in subjective interpretations, or the process of interpretation more generally, even for ostensibly well-defined information.

A variety of analytic traditions are concerned with subjectivity and interpretation, including symbolic interactionism, ethnomethodology, social constructionism, "new ethnography," cultural studies, and some versions of feminism. The active perspective may be adapted to each of these approaches (and others), allowing the investigation of a broad range of research topics and emphases, from the subjective substance of individual's lives and social worlds to the processes of meaning-making.

Sample Selection

Selecting a "sample" for active interviewing is conceived quite differently from sampling done for standard survey research. Traditional approaches target a population in advance, then select individuals who are assumed to be capable of speaking reliably and validly for the population on the basis of their representativeness or informativeness. But, as we suggested in Chapter 3, sampling for an active interview is an ongoing process; designating a group of respondents is tentative, provisional, and sometimes even spontaneous.

Additional respondents, for example, might be added as newly emerging research interests or needs dictate. As interviews reveal particular horizons of meaning associated, say, with different experiential, physical, or cultural locations, the researcher might want to solicit information from an expanded array of people occupying these locations of interest or interpretive significance. The idea is not so much to capture a representative segment of the population as it is to continuously solicit and analyze representative horizons of meaning. In this regard, the "sampling frame," as it were, is meanings—the *whats* of experience—that emerge only through a process of discovery tied to the interviewing itself. This form of active sampling has been described at length by Barney Glaser and Anselm Strauss (1967).

There also is a quite different sense in which sample selection is an ongoing process, centered on the *hows* of meaning-making. This relates in diverse ways to respondents' narrative positioning, communicative context, conversational organization, and multivocality. Respondents are capable of articulating accounts, descriptions, and evaluations in many ways, from more than a single position or perspective, responding in more than one voice, so to speak. Even though the formally designated respondent remains the same, the subject behind the respondent may change virtually from comment to comment. This, of course, has significant implications for just who or what constitutes the sample.

Consider the sampling complications and opportunities encountered in an interview study of the availability and quality of community-based services for persons diagnosed as chronically mentally ill. The study was designed to include a variety of informants from across the community, including representatives of service-providing organizations and agencies, potential clients of those organizations, potential clients' significant others, and other knowledgeable persons. A sample was drawn to obtain these representative viewpoints.

Wellness, Inc., a local self-help group, was one of the community organizations designated as part of the sample. The executive director agreed to act as a respondent, and the interview proceeded smoothly and informatively as she recounted details of the group's mission, membership, resource base, objectives, and the like. Taking the original request to be interviewed as an invitation to speak as the director of the agency and as a group leader, the respondent developed descriptive and evaluative horizons and linkages reflecting the perspective of a service provider.

Midway through the interview, however, the director was asked, "What do clients get out of the group?" Although this was not explicitly anticipated, the question served as an invitation to the respondent to switch interpretive positions. "Speaking as a former mental patient," she began, "I can't tell you how isolated I used to feel before we got the group together." She then proceeded to describe the organization from the perspective of a service recipient.

This repositioning not only introduced a complication of voice but represented a sampling quandary for the researchers. The respondent had been selected as an informant because she was an "organizational administrator"; the data from her interview were to be classified and analyzed as part of the "organizational" sample. With this shift in narrative position, the respondent now became a "client" of the service provision system, not a "provider." Her interview answers seemed absolutely pertinent, but not as part of the original organizational sample. Questions for the researchers now arose: Who was this respondent? In which pile do we place her interview schedule? How should her interview responses be coded? How do we analyze her answers?

The possibility of positional shifts means that sampling can, and does, occur during the interview itself, contributing in the process to what is communicated. When the interviewer explicitly encourages or seeks to clarify such shifts, he or she is, in effect, actively modifying the sample. Similarly, the respondent has a hand in sampling too. Spontaneously deciding to "switch voices," the respondent makes practical and theoretical sampling decisions as well. The sampling process, then, is indigenous and never fully under the control of a sampling design. This is, of course, both a complication and a strength of active sampling; it suggests that sampling as an ongoing activity involving all interview participants—respondents, researchers, and interviewers.

Active Interviewing

Despite its relative flexibility, the active interview is not without organization. As a meaning-making occasion, the active interview is guided by the interviewer and his or her research agenda. The interviewer must therefore be prepared to furnish precedence, incitement, restraint, and perspective as the interview proceeds, not to avoid them.

This begins from the moment that the interview is proposed to the respondent. Introductions and requests to participate should strategically convey the topic areas to be explored and the positions from which the exploration might embark. The researcher's objective is to provide initial contexts for how the respondent might possibly engage the interviewer's inquiries. Although contexts shift throughout the interview, the point of departure must be conscientiously established going in.

The active interview is a conversation, but not without a guiding purpose or plan. As in other interviews, interviewers' questions incite responses that address the researchers' interests. The standard concern for contamination is replaced by the awareness of activeness—both the respondent's and the interviewer's. The point is to capitalize on the dynamic interplay between the two to make reveal both the substance and process of meaning-making in relation to research objectives.

An interview guide can provide the interviewer with a set of predetermined questions that might be used as appropriate to engage the respondent and designate the narrative terrain. In contrast to the standardized questionnaire, which dictates the questions to be asked, the active interview guide is advisory, more of a conversational agenda than a procedural directive. The use of the guide may vary from one interview to the next, becoming the crux of the interview conversation on some occasions and virtually abandoned on others as the respondent (with the interviewer) stakes out and develops narrative territory.

Cultivating the respondent's narrative activity is a paramount goal. The interviewer encourages this at every juncture. This means that the respondent's positional shifts, linkages, and horizons of meaning take precedence over the tacit linkages and horizons of the predesignated questions that the interviewer is prepared to ask. A rule of thumb for using an interview guide is to let the respondent's responses determine whether particular questions are necessary or appropriate as leading frames of reference for the interview conversation. This lends a rather improvisational, yet focused, quality to the interview—precisely the image we have of the meaning-making process more generally.

The active interviewer may interject him- or herself into the interview in various ways, all of which incite or encourage respondents' narratives. Conversational give-and-take around topics of mutual interest is a way of conveying to the respondent that the interviewer is sensitive to, and interested in, the ongoing line of talk. Drawing on mutually familiar events, experiences, or outlooks not only secures rapport or "communion" (as Douglas, 1985, might say) but fixes the conversation on particular horizons of meaning or narrative connections, encouraging the respondent to elaborate.

Background knowledge of circumstances relevant to the research topic and/or the respondent's experience can be an invaluable resource for the interviewer. If possible, active interviewers should be familiar with the material, cultural, and interpretive circumstances to which respondents might orient, and with the vocabulary through which experience will be conveyed. This is important, not only as a means of better understanding respondents' perspectives and interpretations but as a way of cultivating shared awareness and experiences that might be referenced as bases for interview conversations. Background knowledge allows the interviewer to move from the hypothetical or abstract to the very concrete by asking questions about relevant aspects of respondents' lives and experience, a particularly fruitful tactic for promoting circumstantially rich descriptions, accounts, and explanations. The general point is to engage respondents in meaningful talk about their everyday worlds in terms that derive from the circumstances of lived experience (Smith, 1987).

Finally, the active interviewer conscientiously, but cautiously, promotes multivocality. As interactively warranted, the interviewer encourages the respondent to shift narrative positions, to take different roles, throughout the interviewer. Asking the respondent to address a topic from one point of view, then another, is a way of activating the respondent's stock of knowledge, of exploring the various ways that the respondent attaches meaning to the phenomena under investigation. The contradictions and complexities that may emerge from positional shifts are rethought to signal alternative horizons and linkages. Such inconsistencies might vex practitioners of the standardized survey, but they are the stock-in-trade of active interviewing. These procedural considerations all capitalize on the view that meaning is dynamic, actively assembled from complex resources in relation to narrative contexts and circumstances. The tasks of the active interviewer, then, extend far beyond asking a list of questions. It involves encouraging subjective relevancies, prompting interpretive possibilities, facilitating narrative linkages, suggesting alternative perspectives, and appreciating diverse horizons of meaning. Because of this, methods of active interviewing cannot be strictly prescribed. Our suggestions are far from rulelike. Instead, we offer a guiding orientation for interviewing: Make interpretive practice paramount. All strategic considerations follow from this.

Data Collection

Because active interviewing is concerned with meaning and its construction, its data are both substantive and processual. Precoded response formats are decidedly inadequate for capturing the emergent phenomena that the approach generates. Instead, the active interviewer is reconceptualized as something of an "ethnographer of the interview," who records for future analysis not only what is said but the related interactional details of how the interview was accomplished.

If possible, the researcher should audio- or videotape interviews. The tapes can later be transcribed for close analysis. When this is not possible, detailed "process notes" of interview conversations are taken, which should be clarified and elaborated as soon after the completion of the interview as possible. With or without actual recordings, the researcher also records notes of the circumstances surrounding the interview to provide details of the contexts to which the conversation might have been addressed (see Gubrium & Holstein, 1994; Holstein, 1993).

Data from active interviews comprise the myriad things that respondents say and "do with words" to establish the meaningful horizons of their experience. Consequently, data collection attends to capturing the discursive, interactional meaning-making process. Any summaries of respondents' talk should note not only the substance of what was conveyed but the narrative connections, orientations, and dynamics through which substantive meanings were assembled. Signs of confusion, contradiction, ambiguity, and reluctance should also be noted, because problematic conversation often signals occasions where meanings are being examined, reconstituted, or resisted (DeVault, 1990). We should always keep in mind that active interview data are records of interpretive practice; they capture how things were said as much as what was said.

Analysis and Presentation

Finally, given the unconventional nature of active interviewing, how does one make sense of its data? Analyzing data concerning interpretive practice is somewhat less "scientific" and somewhat more "artful" than conventional interview analysis. This does not mean, however, that analysis is any less rigorous; quite to the contrary, active interview data require attention and sensitivity to both process and substance.

Interviews are conventionally analyzed as descriptions of experience, as more or less accurate reports or representations (literally, representations) of reality. Analysis amounts to systematically grouping and summarizing the descriptions, and providing a coherent organizing framework that encapsulates and explains aspects of the social world that respondents portray. Respondents' interpretive activity is subordinated to the substance of what they report; objective *whats* overwhelm the *hows*.

In contrast, active interview data are analyzed to show the dynamic interrelatedness of the *what* and the *how*. Respondents' talk is not viewed as a collection of reality reports delivered from a fixed repository. Instead, the talk is considered for the ways that it assembles aspects of reality in collaboration with the interviewer. The focus is as much on the assembly process as on what is assembled. Using sociologically oriented forms of narrative and discourse analysis, conversational records of interpretive practice are examined to reveal reality-constructing practices as well as the subjective meanings that are circumstantially conveyed (see DeVault, 1990; Gubrium & Holstein, 1994; Holstein & Gubrium, 1994). The goal is to show how interview responses are produced in the interaction between interviewer and respondent, without losing sight of the meanings produced or the circumstances that condition the meaning-making process. The analytic objective is not merely to describe the situated production of talk but to show how what is being said relates to the experiences and lives being studied.

Writing and presenting findings from interview data is itself an analytically active enterprise. Rather than simply letting the data "speak for themselves," the active analyst empirically documents the meaning-making process. With ample illustration and reference to records of talk, the analyst describes the complex discursive activities through which respondents produce meaning. The goal is to explicate how meanings, their linkages and horizons, are actively constituted within the interview environment, which, as we noted at the start, is an increasingly prevalent "window on the world." Analysts' reports do not summarize and organize what interview participants have said as much as they "deconstruct" participants' talk, showing the reader the *hows* of the *whats* of the narrative dramas of lived experience.

REFERENCES

Abel, E. K. (1991). *Who cares for the elderly?* Philadelphia: Temple University Press.
Alasuutari, P. (1995). *Researching culture: Qualitative method and cultural studies.* London: Sage.
Atkinson, P. (1990). *The ethnographic imagination.* London: Routledge.
Backstrom, C. H., & Hursh, G. (1963). *Survey research.* Evanston, IL: Northwestern University Press.
Bakhtin, M. (1981). *The dialogical principle.* Austin: University of Texas Press.
Bauman, R. (1986). *Story, performance, and event: Contextual studies of oral narrative.* New York: Cambridge University Press.
Behar, R. (1993). *Translated woman: Crossing the border with Esperanza's story.* Boston: Beacon.
Berger, P. L., & Luckmann, T. (1967). *The social construction of reality.* New York: Doubleday.
Blumer, H. (1969). *Symbolic interactionism.* New York: Prentice Hall.
Briggs, C. (1986). *Learning how to ask: A sociolinguistic appraisal of the role of the interviewer in social science research.* Cambridge, UK: Cambridge University Press.
Bruner, J. (1986). *Actual minds, possible worlds.* Cambridge, MA: Harvard University Press.
Burgos-Debray, E. (Ed.). (1984). *I, Rigoberta Menchu.* London: Verso.
Cannell, C. F., Fisher, G., & Marquis, K. H. (1968). *The influence of interviewer and respondent psychological and behavioral variables on the reporting in household interviews* (Vital and Health Statistics, Series 2, No. 26). Washington, DC: Government Printing Office.
Center for Political Studies. (1992). *American National Election Survey.* Ann Arbor: University of Michigan, Institute for Social Research, Center for Political Studies.
Cicourel, A. V. (1964). *Method and measurement in sociology.* New York: Free Press.
Cicourel, A. V. (1974). *Theory and method in a study of Argentine fertility.* New York: John Wiley.
Clifford, J. (1992). Traveling cultures. In L. Grossberg, C. Nelson, & P. Treishler (Eds.), *Cultural studies* (pp. 96-112). New York: Routledge.
Clifford, J., & Marcus, G. E. (Eds.). (1986). *Writing culture.* Berkeley: University of California Press.
Clough, P. T. (1992). *The end(s) of ethnography.* Newbury Park, CA: Sage.
Converse, J. M., & Schuman, H. (1974). *Conversations at random: Survey research as interviewers see it.* New York: John Wiley.
Danziger, K. (1990). *Constructing the subject.* New York: Cambridge University Press.
DeVault, M. (1990). Talking and listening from women's standpoint: Feminist strategies for interviewing and analysis. *Social Problems, 37,* 96-117.
DeVault, M. L. (1991). *Feeding the family: The social organization of caring as gendered work.* Chicago: University of Chicago Press.
Dillman, D. A. (1978). *Mail and telephone surveys.* New York: John Wiley.
Douglas, J. D. (1985). *Creative interviewing.* Beverly Hills, CA: Sage.
Fonow, M. M., & Cook, J. (Eds.). (1991). *Beyond methodology: Feminist scholarship as lived research.* Bloomington: Indiana University Press.

82

Foucault, M. (1979). *Discipline and punish.* New York: Vintage.

Fowler, F. J., & Mangione, T. W. (1990). *Standardized survey interviewing.* Newbury Park, CA: Sage.

Garfinkel, H. (1967). *Studies in ethnomethodology.* Englewood Cliffs, NJ: Prentice Hall.

Geertz, C. (1988). *Works and lives.* Stanford, CA: Stanford University Press.

Glaser, B., & Strauss, A. (1967). *The discovery of grounded theory.* Chicago: Aldine.

Gilligan, C. (1982). *In a different voice.* Cambridge, MA: Harvard University Press.

Gorden, R. L. (1987). *Interviewing: Strategy, techniques, and tactics.* Homewood, IL: Dorsey.

Gubrium, J. F. (1986). *Oldtimers and Alzheimer's.* Greenwich, CT: JAI.

Gubrium, J. F. (1988). *Analyzing field reality.* Newbury Park, CA: Sage.

Gubrium, J. F. (1989). Local cultures and service policy. In J. F. Gubrium & D. Silverman (Eds.), *The politics of field research* (pp. 94-112). London: Sage.

Gubrium, J. F. (1992). *Out of control.* Newbury Park, CA: Sage.

Gubrium, J. F. (1993). *Speaking of life: Horizons of meaning for nursing home residents.* Hawthorne, NY: Aldine de Gruyter.

Gubrium, J. F., & Buckholdt, D. R. (1982). *Describing care.* Cambridge, MA: Oelgeschlager, Gunn and Hain.

Gubrium, J. F., & Holstein, J. A. (1990). *What is family?* Mountain View, CA: Mayfield.

Gubrium, J. F., & Holstein, J. A. (1994). Analyzing talk and interaction. In J. Gubrium & A. Sankar (Eds.), *Qualitative methods in aging research* (pp. 173-188). Thousand Oaks, CA: Sage.

Gubrium, J. F., & Holstein, J. A. (1995). Biographical work and new ethnography. In R. Josselson & A. Lieblich (Eds.), *The narrative study of lives* (Vol. 3). Thousand Oaks, CA: Sage.

Gubrium, J. F., Holstein, J. A., & Buckholdt, D. R. (1994). *Constructing the life course.* Dix Hills, NY: General Hall.

Harding, S. (Ed.). (1987). *Feminism and methodology.* Bloomington: Indiana University Press.

Heritage, J. (1984). *Garfinkel and ethnomethodology.* Cambridge, UK: Polity.

Holstein, J. A. (1988). Court-ordered incompetence: Conversational organization in involuntary commitment proceedings. *Social Problems, 35,* 458-473.

Holstein, J. A. (1993). *Court-ordered insanity: Interpretive practice and involuntary commitment.* Hawthorne, NY: Aldine de Gruyter.

Holstein, J. A., & Gubrium, J. F. (1994). Phenomenology, ethnomethodology, and interpretive practice. In N. K. Denzin & Y. Lincoln (Eds.), *Handbook of qualitative research* (pp. 262-272). Thousand Oaks, CA: Sage.

Holstein, J. A., & Staples, W. G. (1992). Producing evaluative knowledge: The interactional bases of social science findings. *Sociological Inquiry, 62,* 11-35.

Hyman, H. H., Cobb, W. J., Feldman, J. J., Hart, C. W., & Stember, C. H. (1975). *Interviewing in social research.* Chicago: University of Chicago Press.

Institute for Survey Research. (1987). *National Survey of Families and Households.* Philadelphia, PA: Temple University, Institute for Survey Research.

Johnson, J. C. (1990). *Selecting ethnographic informants.* Newbury Park, CA: Sage.

Jones, M. O., Moore, M. D., & Snyder, R. C. (Eds.). (1988). *Inside organizations.* Newbury Park, CA: Sage.

83

Kimmel, D. C. (1974). *Adulthood and aging.* New York: John Wiley.

Kirk, J., & Miller, M. L. (1986). *Reliability and validity in qualitative research.* Beverly Hills, CA: Sage.

Maccoby, E. E., & Maccoby, N. (1954). The interview: A tool of social science. In G. Lindzey (Ed.), *Handbook of social psychology* (pp. 449-487). Reading, MA: Addison-Wesley.

Madge, J. (1965). *The tools of social science.* Garden City, NY: Anchor.

Manning, P. L. (1967). Problems in interpreting interview data. *Sociology and Social Research, 51,* 301-316.

Marcus, G., & Fischer, M. (1986). *Anthropology as cultural critique.* Chicago: University of Chicago Press.

Mayhew, H. (1861-1862). *London labour and the London poor.* London: Griffin, Bohn and Company.

Mishler, E. G. (1986). *Research interviewing.* Cambridge, MA: Harvard University Press.

Mishler, E. G. (1991). Representing discourse: The rhetoric of transcription. *Journal of Narrative and Life History, 1,* 255-280.

Morgan, D. L. (1988). *Focus groups as qualitative research.* Newbury Park, CA: Sage.

Moser, C. A. (1958). *Survey methods in social investigation.* London: Heinemann.

Myerhoff, B. (1992). *Remembered lives.* Ann Arbor: University of Michigan Press.

Ochberg, R. L. (1994). Life stories and storied lives. In A. Lieblich & R. Josselson (Eds.), *The narrative study of lives* (Vol. 2, pp. 113-144). Thousand Oaks, CA: Sage.

Opie, A. (1994). The instability of the caring body: Gender and caregivers of confused older people. *Qualitative Health Research, 4,* 31-50.

Pollner, M. (1987). *Mundane reason.* Cambridge, UK: Cambridge University Press.

Pool, I. de S. (1957). A critique of the twentieth anniversary issue. *Public Opinion Quarterly, 21,* 190-198.

Rabinow, P. (1977). *Reflections on fieldwork in Morocco.* Berkeley: University of California Press.

Reinharz, S. (1992). *Feminist methods of social research.* New York: Oxford University Press.

Riessman, C. K. (1993). *Narrative analysis.* Newbury Park, CA: Sage.

Rogers, C. R. (1945). The non-directive method as a technique for social research. *American Journal of Sociology, 50,* 279-283.

Sacks, H., Schegloff, E., & Jefferson, G. (1974). A simplest systematics for the organization of turn-taking in conversation. *Language, 50,* 696-735.

Sarbin, T. R. (1986). *Narrative psychology: The storied nature of human conduct.* New York: Praeger.

Schütz, A. (1967). *The phenomenology of the social world.* Evanston, IL: Northwestern University Press.

Silverman, D. (1985). *Qualitative method and sociology.* Aldershot, UK: Gower.

Silverman, D. (1989). The impossible dreams of reformism and romanticism. In J. F. Gubrium & D. Silverman (Eds.), *The politics of field research* (pp. 30-48). London: Sage.

Silverman, D. (1993). *Kundera's immortality and field research: Uncovering the romantic impulse.* Unpublished manuscript, Department of Sociology, Goldsmith's College, University of London.

Silverman, D. (1994). *Interpreting qualitative data*. London: Sage.

Smith, D. E. (1987). *The everyday world as problematic: A feminist sociology*. Boston: Northeastern University Press.

Smith, D. E. (1990). *Texts, facts, and femininity*. New York: Routledge.

Stanley, L. (1983). *Breaking out: Feminist consciousness and feminist research*. London: Routledge.

Sudman, S., & Bradburn, N. M. (1983). *Asking questions*. San Francisco: Jossey-Bass.

Taylor, C. (1989). *Sources of the self*. Cambridge, MA: Harvard University Press.

Terkel, S. (1972). *Working*. New York: Avon.

Thorne, B. (1993). *Gender play*. New Brunswick, NJ: Rutgers University Press.

Thorne, B., Kramarae, C., & Henley, N. (Eds.). (1983). *Language, gender, and society*. New York: Newbury House.

Todorov, T. (1984). *Mikhail Bakhtin: The dialogical principle*. Minneapolis: University of Minnesota Press.

Van Maanen, J. (1988). *Tales of the field*. Chicago: University of Chicago Press.

Williams, R. (1993). Culture is ordinary. In A. Gray & J. McGuigan (Eds.), *Studying culture* (pp. 5-41). London: Edward Arnold. (Original work published 1958)

Willis, P. (1990). *Common culture*. Boulder, CO: Westview.

ABOUT THE AUTHORS

JAMES A. HOLSTEIN is Professor of Sociology at Marquette University. He brings an ethnomethodologically informed constructionist perspective to research in a variety of areas, including mental health and illness, social problems, family studies, and the life course. He is author of *Court-Ordered Insanity: Interpretive Practice and Involuntary Commitment* (1993), and coeditor of *Reconsidering Social Constructionism* (1993) and *Constructionist Controversies* (1993). He also edits the research annual *Perspectives on Social Problems*.

JABER F. GUBRIUM is Professor of Sociology at the University of Florida. He has conducted research on the social organization of care in diverse treatment settings, from nursing homes and physical rehabilitation to counseling and family therapy. His continuing fieldwork on the organizational embeddedness of experience serves as a basis for comparative, interpretive ethnography. He is editor of *Journal of Aging Studies* and author of *Living and Dying at Murray Manor* (1975), *Oldtimers and Alzheimer's* (1986), *Analyzing Field Reality* (1988), *Out of Control* (1992), and *Speaking of Life: Horizons of Meaning for Nursing Home Residents* (1993).

Holstein and Gubrium have developed their distinctive constructionist perspective in a variety of collaborative projects, including *What Is Family?* (1990) and *Constructing the Life Course* (1994). They are currently analyzing families with recently institutionalized members, focusing on interpretive practice at the family-institution nexus. They are also working on a more extensive theoretical and methodological perspective on the new language of qualitative method.